Anahita's Portfolio

Combining Artists and Civil Rights Leaders

By Fiona McCargo

Author's Note

Anahita's Portfolio is a fictional work based on historical facts and artists. The drawings and story are based on art and on the Author's imagination to engage the reader.

Thank you to my friends and family for their input on Anahita's Portfolio.

ISBN-13: 978-1518711268

ISBN-10: 151871126X

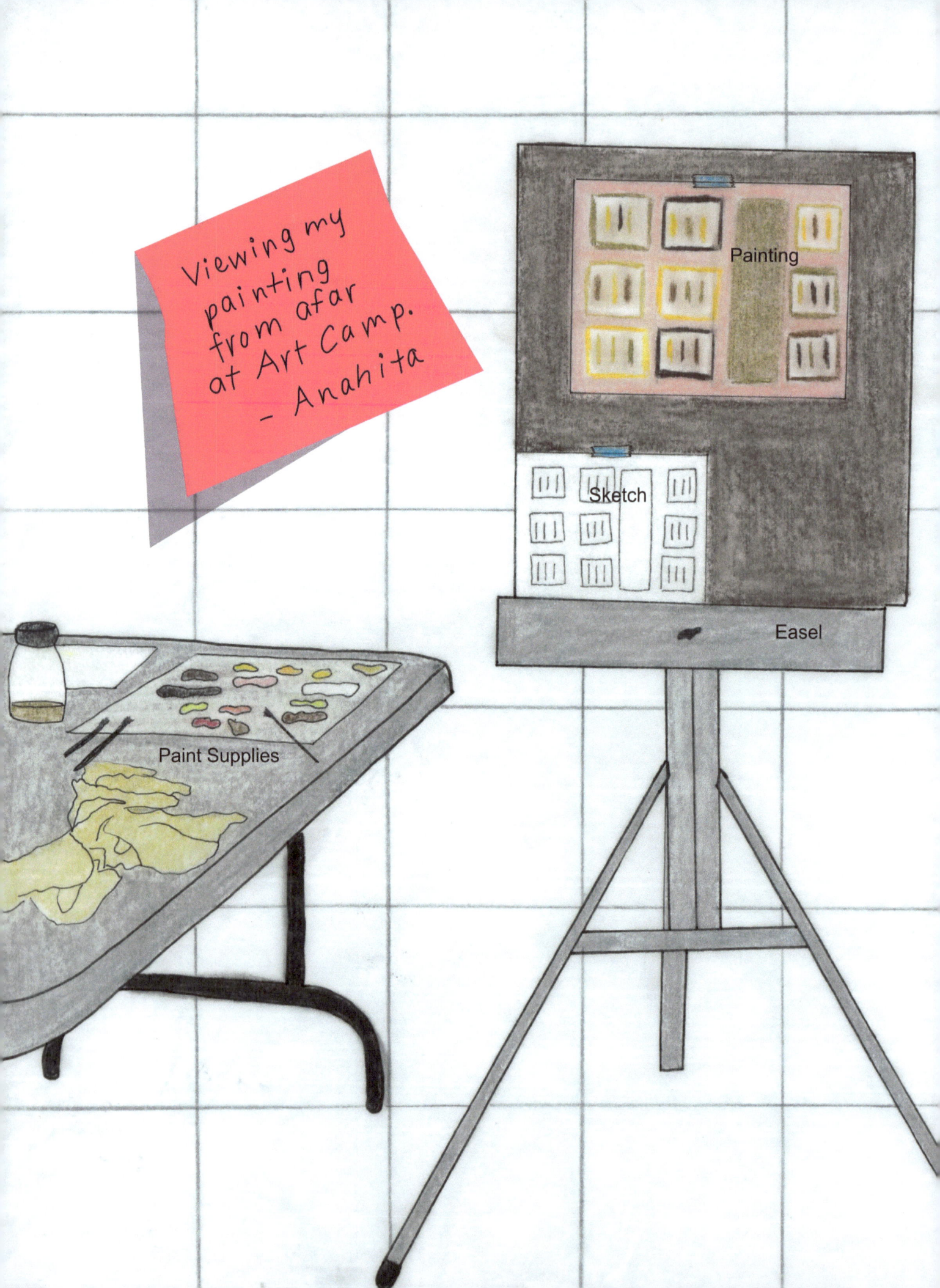

MY VISION

- CAN THE VIEWER EASILY UNDERSTAND MY VISION?
- ENGAGE THE VIEWER WITH MY VISION
- STATE GOALS CLEARLY
- HAVE A CONSISTENT VISION THROUGHOUT PORTFOLIO

This is my mom, Kimiya. She came home from her job as an architect with an Art Camp flyer and asked me if I want to apply. If I apply, then Mom will help me because she applies for architecture competitions and knows that little mistakes can make a big difference in whether she wins.

I read through the flyer and decided that I would love to go to Art Camp. One of my goals is to be an artist and this will help me to create a body of work, to enhance my skills, and to learn about art and history. I plan to apply right away since the deadline is approaching!

Mom suggested that I get some library books about people who interest me. Right now, I want to know more about Leaders in the Civil Rights Movement. These people seem rather old to me so Mom said I have to make them jump off the page.

Mom

Apply for Art Camp!

Submit a portfolio showing your artistic abilities as they relate to historical figures.

Use the portfolio to show us who you are and how this camp will help you in your artistic pursuits or education.

Eligibility: Must be nine to twelve years old with parental permission.

Deadline: April 5th.

Application: Submit portfolio or go online at:

Me

- MAKE THE PORTFOLIO SPECIFIC TO THE AUDIENCE

  EXAMPLE: ART CAMP EMPLOYEES

- FOLLOW ANY GUIDELINES

  EXAMPLE: PAGE SIZES, MAXIMUM PAGES, BINDING OPTIONS, AND MATERIALS

Then Mom asked about the type of art that I want to portray. I have so many interests. Mom is from Iran and I have some favorite Iranian artists. Dad is African American and I want to include some of those artists as well. I like Native American art and Mexican art. I should include some of the more prominent artists in Surrealism, Impressionism, Cubism and so on.

HISTORY
• AFRICAN-AMERICANS

ART
• ARTISTS
• ART STYLES

DESIGN
• LAYOUT
• UNIFORMITY

I have so much work to do. I should get started! Once I have all the pages, Mom will help me to organize and review them to make sure they are consistent and coherent. They will be coherent when they all meet in the middle like my arrows suggest; where art, history, and design converge with equal weight given to each topic.

I can either submit my portfolio electronically or I can make the portfolio by hand or on the computer and print it out. If I make a paper application, then I have to consider many aspects including how long it will take to mail my booklet.

Me

- CHOOSE A VISIBLE OR INVISIBLE GRID

- BE CONSISTENT UNLESS DELIBERATELY MAKING A STATEMENT

- IS ONE COLUMN ALWAYS USED FOR TEXT?

- USE A GRID TO POSITION TEXT, IMAGES, AND BLANK SPACE

1   When I am sketching, I have to consider how my design will look on each page. Using my fingers to show the grids, or ways to break up space on the paper, I have about six grids. The grids are in orange. How do I use the space wisely?

I need to leave space for both images and text. If I have too much text, then no one will want to read what I wrote no matter how well it is written. If I have too many images, then there is no content. The one exception would be if I had one of the facing pages with lots of text while the other page had images.

In order to connect with my reader, I need to think about who will be reading my submission. Who is my audience? Is my audience also in the nine to twelve year old range? Is my audience an adult who works at the camp and who loves art? Is my audience an employee at the art camp who makes decisions about which children can attend the camp, but who may not love art?

To have a strong portfolio I have to establish these relationships:
- between myself and the reader
- between each page
- between the Artists and Civil Rights Leaders
- between art and politics
- between the pages as they progress to the end
- between the portfolio set up (such as a fold out page) and the content (such as a reason to have a fold out page)

2

I should start by choosing a basic format for my sketches. I could use a portrait or landscape page.   I chose a portrait.

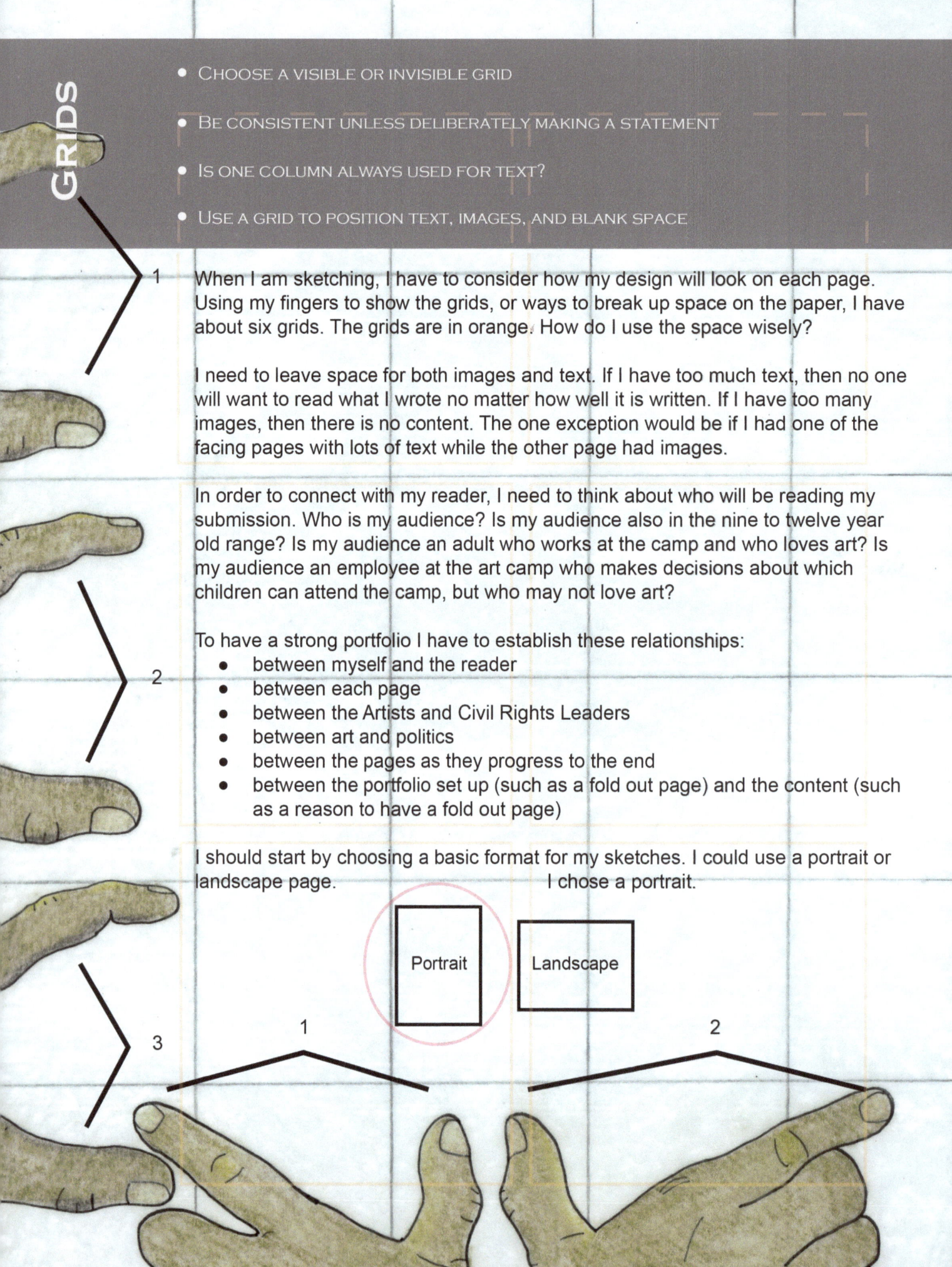

Portrait

Landscape

1

2

3

- CHOOSE A COMBINATION OF PAPER, BINDING, AND ELECTRONIC DESIGN

- DECIDE ON THE RHYTHM THAT WILL ATTRACT THE EYE

- USE ELEMENTS TO MAKE A BEAUTIFUL PORTFOLIO

- CUT OUT ITEMS THAT DO NOT FIT YOUR VISION OR THEME

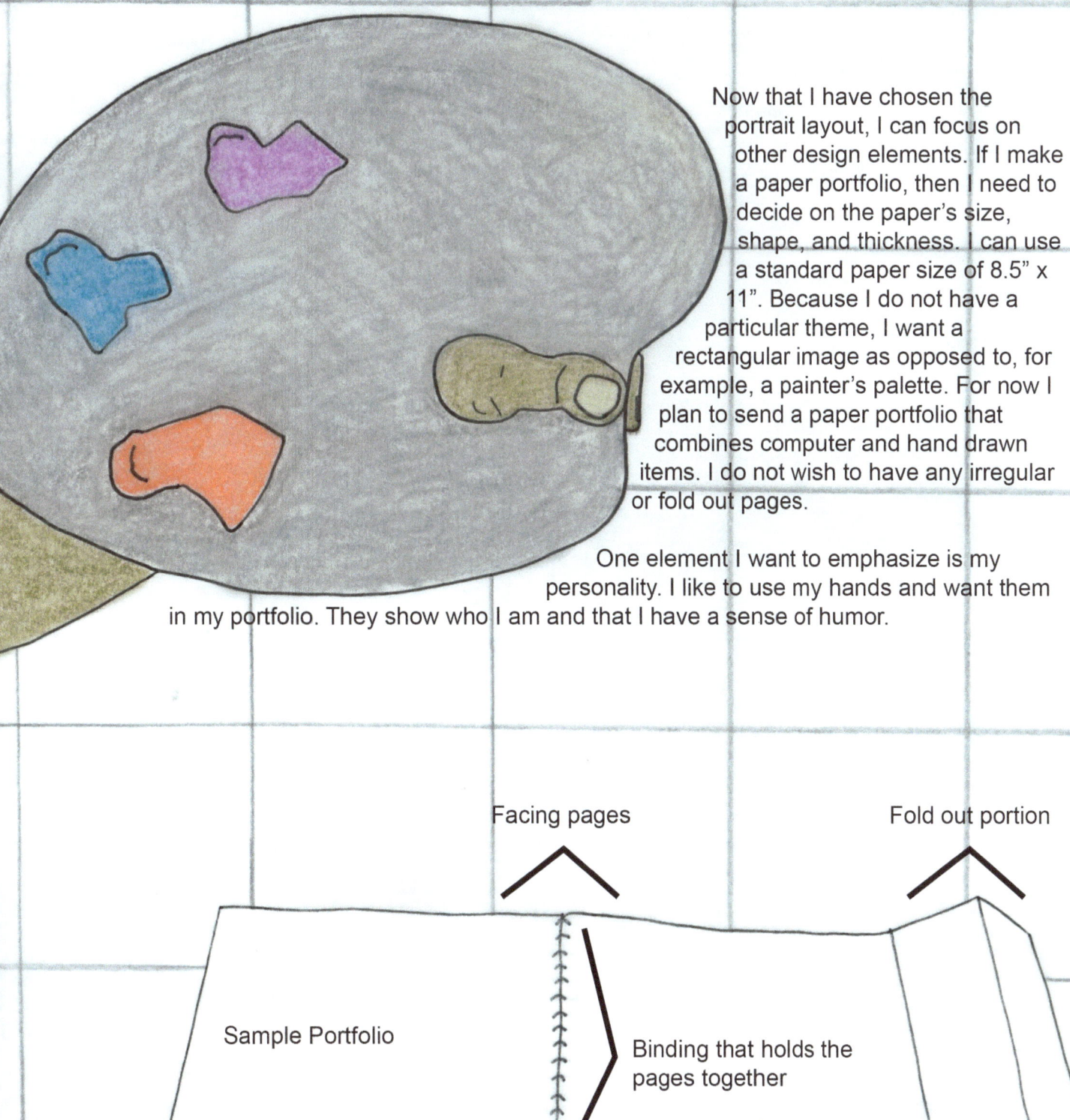

Now that I have chosen the portrait layout, I can focus on other design elements. If I make a paper portfolio, then I need to decide on the paper's size, shape, and thickness. I can use a standard paper size of 8.5" x 11". Because I do not have a particular theme, I want a rectangular image as opposed to, for example, a painter's palette. For now I plan to send a paper portfolio that combines computer and hand drawn items. I do not wish to have any irregular or fold out pages.

One element I want to emphasize is my personality. I like to use my hands and want them in my portfolio. They show who I am and that I have a sense of humor.

Facing pages

Fold out portion

Sample Portfolio

Binding that holds the pages together

I tend to choose a font because it is pleasing to me and easy to read. To separate ideas, I can use different sizes of fonts. If I were to suddenly write in this font, or a **bold** font, the reader might wonder why I changed the text.

Text is important but images are the heart of my portfolio. My images need to be in focus unless I want them to be harder to see. Images should have high resolution. For instance, I will scan my portfolio images at 600 dpi (dots per inch). The more dots there are in an inch, the better the image will look.

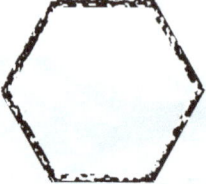 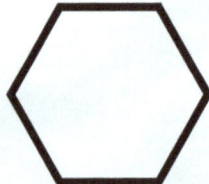

The image above does not have clear edges. It is out of focus, and harder to see.

The image above has clear and defined edges. It is easy to see.

Once all of the images are done, it is necessary to order them based on facing pages as well as impact and storyline. I need to ask what images look good together and why. When the pages are bound together, the images and text should be visible and the binding should hold up over time.

How should I order these and my other images?

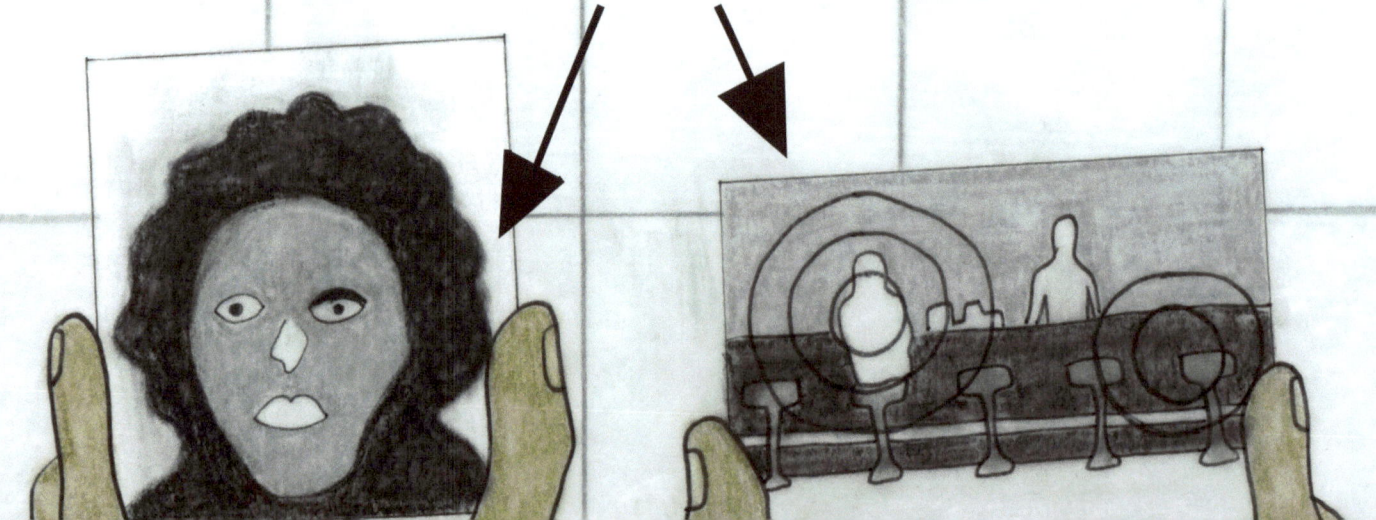

- Put an image on one page or across two pages (called facing pages)

- Show story or narrative

- Use colors to navigate booklet

- Move from black and white images to color if appropriate

On my computer I researched Civil Rights Leaders and Artists. I created a spreadsheet showing the Civil Rights Leaders on the left with the men followed by the women. Under the Artists' column I have the Artist that I will pair with each Leader. My plan is to make a drawing of the Leader in an art style similar to the artist that I paired him or her with so that I can show my artistic talents. This will allow me to dynamically write about the connection of art and history, and art and politics in order to get interested in the art, to interest others in my portfolio, and to get into the Art Camp.

Civil Rights Leaders		Artists	
James Lawson	b. 1928	William H Johnson	b. 1901
Pierre Caliste Landry	b. 1841	Roger de La Fresnaye	b. 1885
P B S Pinchback	b. 1837	Ernst Kirchner	b. 1880
Blanche Kelso Bruce	b. 1841	Chuck Close	b. 1940
Huey Percy Newton	b. 1942	Shirin Neshat	b. 1957
Medgar Evers	b. 1925	Jackson Pollock	b. 1912
George McLaurin	b. 1887	Remedios Varo	b. 1908
James Weldon Johnson	b. 1871	Henri Matisse	b. 1869
W E B Du Bois	b. 1868	Bob Haozous	b. 1943
James Meredith	b. 1933	R C Gorman	b. 1932
Bernard Layfayette	b. 1940	Palmer Hayden	b. 1890
James Chaney	b. 1943	Lois Mailou Jones	b. 1905
Ella Baker	b. 1903	Francis Picabia	b. 1879
Ida B Wells	b. 1862	Forough Yavari	b. 1978
Fannie Lou Hamer	b. 1917	Fritz Scholder	b. 1937
Vivian Malone	b. 1942	Frida Kahlo	b. 1907
Dorothy Bell	~b. 1944	Aaron Douglas	b. 1899
Constance Baker Motley	b. 1921	Georges Seurat	b. 1859
Minnijean Brown	b. 1941	Diego Rivera	b. 1886
Diane Nash	b. 1938	Jacob Lawrence	b. 1917

This is my completed portfolio.

Turn the page for what is inside!

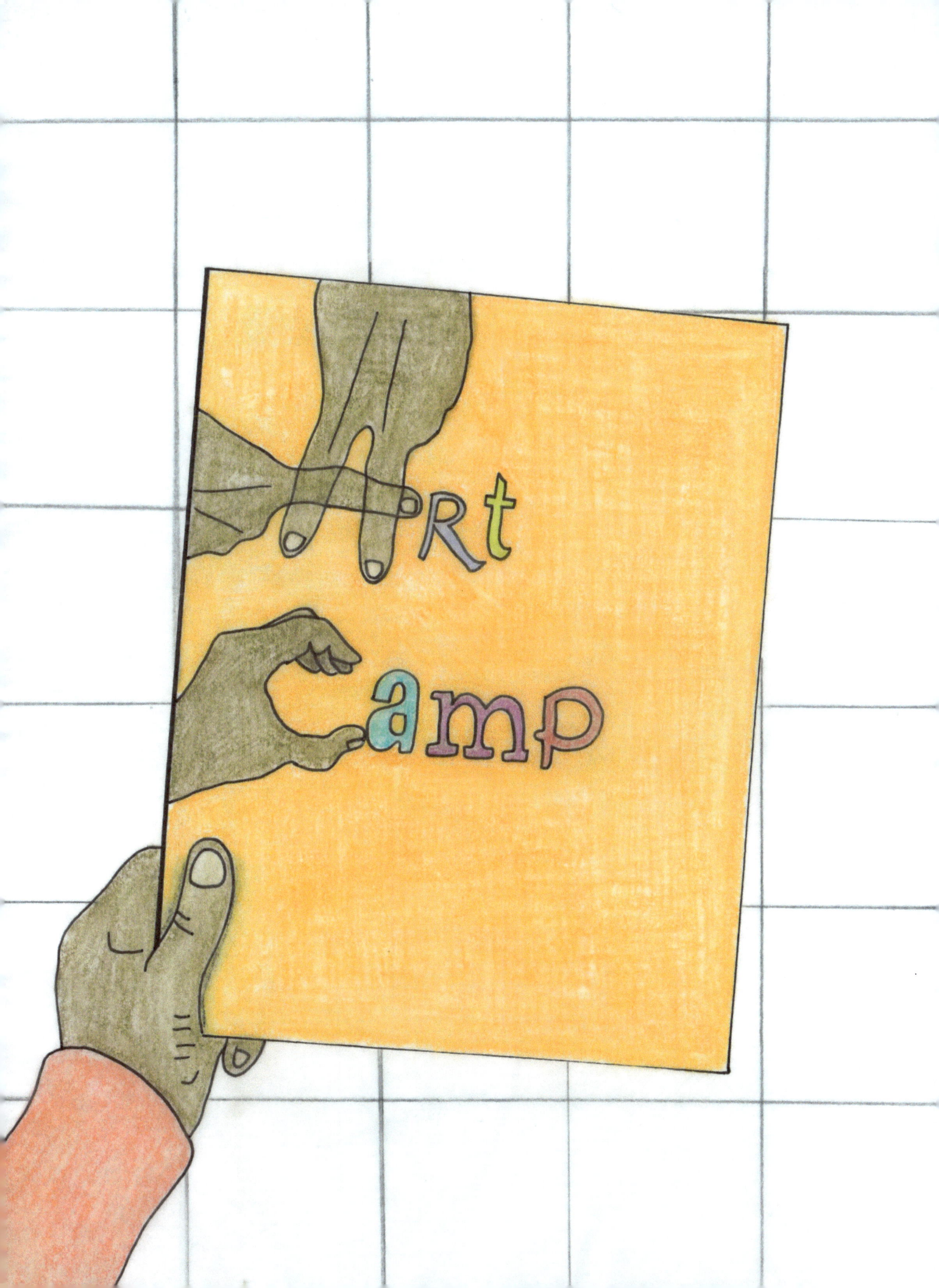

I selected this drawing of Fannie Lou Hamer as my first Leader in a style by Native American Artist Fritz Scholder because both were interested in change. In particular I chose Fritz as my first Artist because he went to Art Camp around age eighteen where he was both President and Best Boy Artist.

Fannie was born a slave in Mississippi and when slaves were freed, she and her husband worked on a plantation in return for a portion of the crops. At 44 years old she was helped by Charles McLaurin to take a test to become a registered voter. The plantation owner came to stop her. She took the test and moved out of the plantation to avoid being shot. She helped others to claim their rights to vote and spoke at the Credentials Committee Hearing in Atlantic City even though President Johnson tried to call a conference to detract media attention.

I created a representation of Fannie in Fritz's Colorist style. I am blending the colors in a diagonal fashion using my hand.

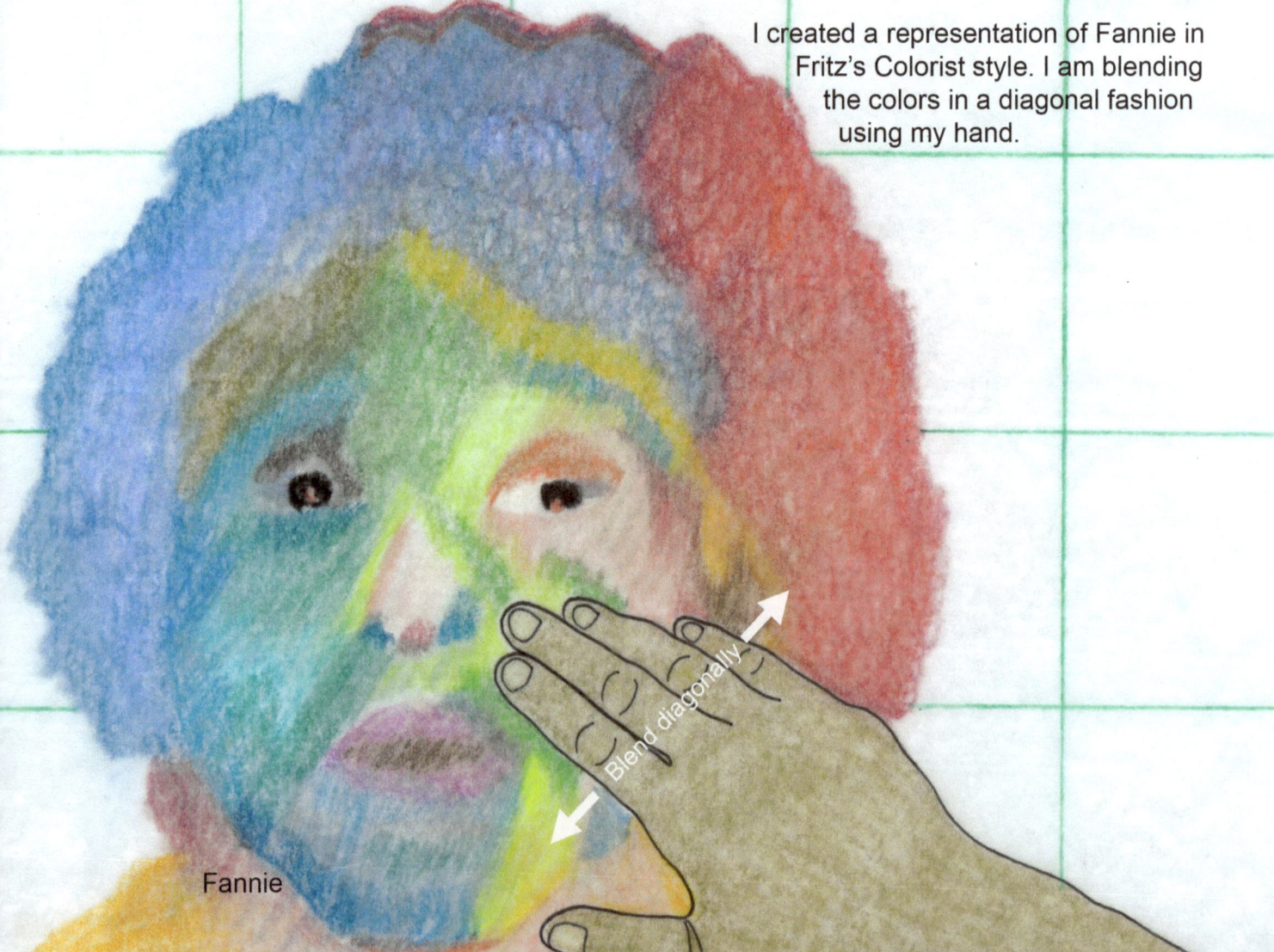

Blend diagonally

Fannie

- BELIEVED HE WOULD BE SUCCESSFUL

- LIKED TAOS VALLEY BECAUSE OF ITS LANDSCAPE, ART, AND SPIRIT

- WORKED IN MANY ART FORMS

- RECEIVED THE GOVERNOR'S AWARD OF EXCELLENCE IN NEW MEXICO

The Leader J H Meredith is shown in the Abstract Realist style of Artist and Native American R C Gorman. I combined these people because both believed in themselves enough to help them make money and have successful lives.

J H was born into a poor Mississippi family. His dad named him J H but when he joined the Air Force, J H had to choose names; he called himself James Howard. When he left the Air Force, J H went to Jackson State College, an African American school, but wanted to transfer to the University of Mississippi, a school with only Caucasians. He got help from Medgar Evers and Constance Baker Motely who worked for the National Association for the Advancement of Colored People (NAACP) that helped all individuals to have the same rights. The Governor and Lieutenant Governor continued to try to stop J H. Because of President Kennedy's negotiations, and with over 500 federal marshals, James was allowed to attend. He graduated from the University. He went on to law school at Columbia University.

I created James in an abstract version where I blended from side to side the white marks that appear to both blind and protect him.

← Blend\horizontally →

James or J H

I chose to combine the Leader W E B Du Bois with the Modern Artist Bob Haozous because both did not like injustice.

W E B was born free. His family had been free for 100 years. W E B went to Fisk University and then to Harvard. At Harvard he was the first African American to earn a Doctorate. W E B was a teacher at Atlanta University and at the University of Pennsylvania. He wrote about racial injustice and the need for African Americans to get good educations in order to lead others. He wrote essays. As one of the people who started the NAACP, W E B was the editor of a monthly magazine called *The Crisis*. W E B used *The Crisis* to write about issues that angered him and therefore he did not get along well with others.

Because W E B spoke out against Jim Crow laws (that kept African Americans separate from Caucasians until 1965), I put images of crows and "CROW" in the art. This is contrasted to Bob's work where he used images of chickens implying that the Native American he was representing was that bird.

CROW

CROW

CROW

WEB

- CREATED MURALS THAT SHOW A TIMELINE FROM LIFE IN AFRICA WITH DRUMS TO SEGREGATION IN THE UNITED STATES TO THE GREAT MIGRATION NORTHWARD

- USED MUSIC, MYTHOLOGY, RELIGION, AND POLITICS IN HIS ART

- WORKED IN A PRECISIONIST STYLE

AARON DOUGLAS

Leader Dorothy Bell is paired with Artist Aaron Douglas. I chose this combination because Dorothy participated in politics and Aaron made art about the same topic.

In Birmingham, Alabama, Dorothy was a college student who sat at lunch counters to occupy seats with the hope of getting served by Caucasian wait staff. The year was 1963. She practiced nonviolent sit-ins and was arrested many times.

I show Dorothy seated at the lunch counter waiting for service that will never come. She is at the heart of the set of circles because I want to focus on the injustice she is experiencing. The other circle is on the empty stool to show that even with no one at the counter, Dorothy will not get any food.

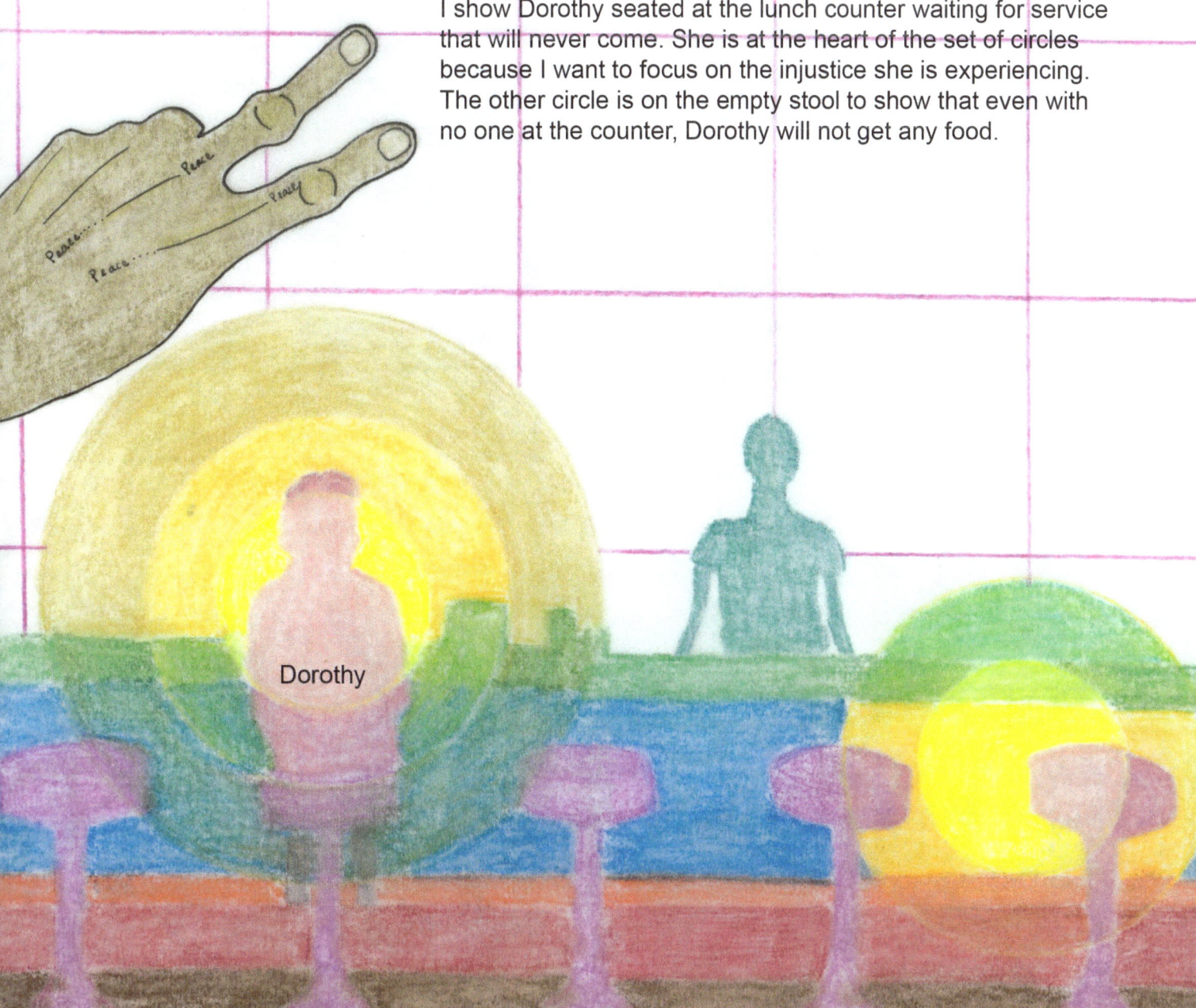

Dorothy

PALMER HAYDEN

- STUDIED IN PARIS

- MADE ART THAT SHOWED EVERYDAY SOCIAL LIFE IN HARLEM AND IN THE SOUTH

- CREATED AFRICAN AMERICANS WITH LARGE LIPS AND BIG ROUND HEADS CAUSING CRITICS TO QUESTION IF HE WAS MAKING ART FOR CAUCASIANS TO BUY

The Leader Bernard Lafayette is drawn in the style of Artist Palmer Hayden. I combined these people because Bernard participated in everyday events to desegregate the South and Palmer made images about everyday activities.

Bernard was a member of the Student Nonviolent Coordinating Committee (SNCC). Ellla Baker helped to start the SNCC in the 1960s. The people who worked and volunteered for the SNCC would stage sit-ins at restaurants and would ride buses (called Freedom Rides) through the South where it was illegal for African Americans and Caucasians to be on the same buses or in the same bus terminals. Bernard did not fight back when people hit him because he used nonviolence just as the Indian leader Gandhi. He helped to organize voting rights for all people in Selma, Alabama. During his protests, he was arrested 27 times.

I am showing Bernard by an image of the United States with some locations where Freedom Riders rode buses because when they got off the buses, they were often arrested or harmed. He is in the style of Palmer's art because many Caucasians did not think that African Americans were their equals.

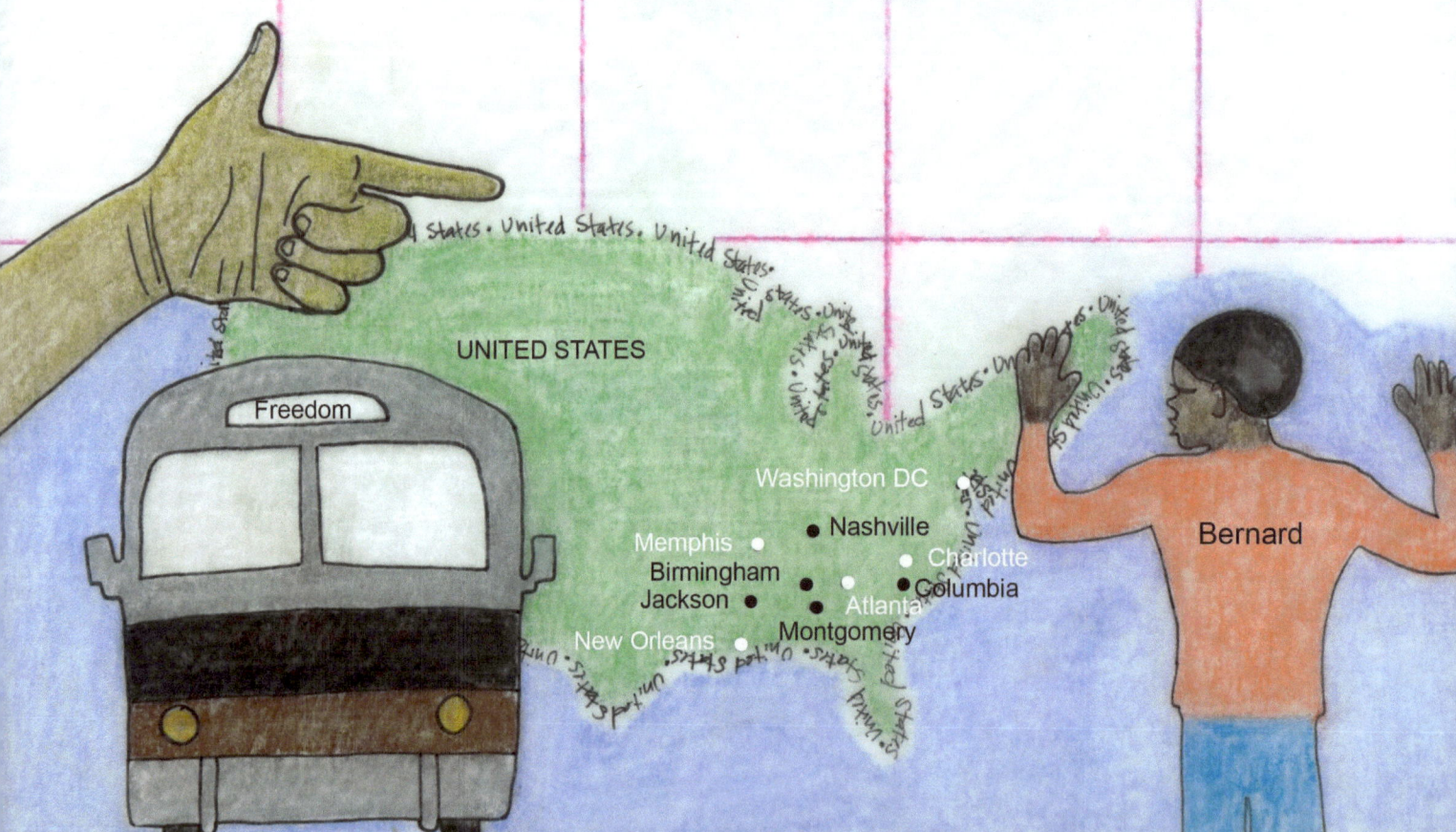

- USED REALISM AND PRIMITIVISM TO SHOW PEOPLE IN HIS ART WORK

- MADE ART IN PRIMITIVE, BASIC, AND CHILDLIKE MANNERS

- SHOWED RELIGIOUS SCENES

- STUDIED AT THE NATIONAL ACADEMY OF DESIGN

James Lawson was a Leader who also practiced nonviolence like Gandhi. I drew James in a style similar to that of Artist William H Johnson because they were both deliberately making decisions.

James learned of Gandhi's teachings when he was in Nagpur, India. Before going to India, he became a preacher and went to college in Ohio. Because he refused to go into the military, he went to jail for several years. After his stay in India, James met Martin Luther King, Jr., and he spread the word about nonviolent ways to change the laws so that everyone could be equal.

I drew James with halos because he was a preacher. He is shown in a simplistic manner so that the focus is on him. Traveling to India made an impact on his life therefore I included India in this image.

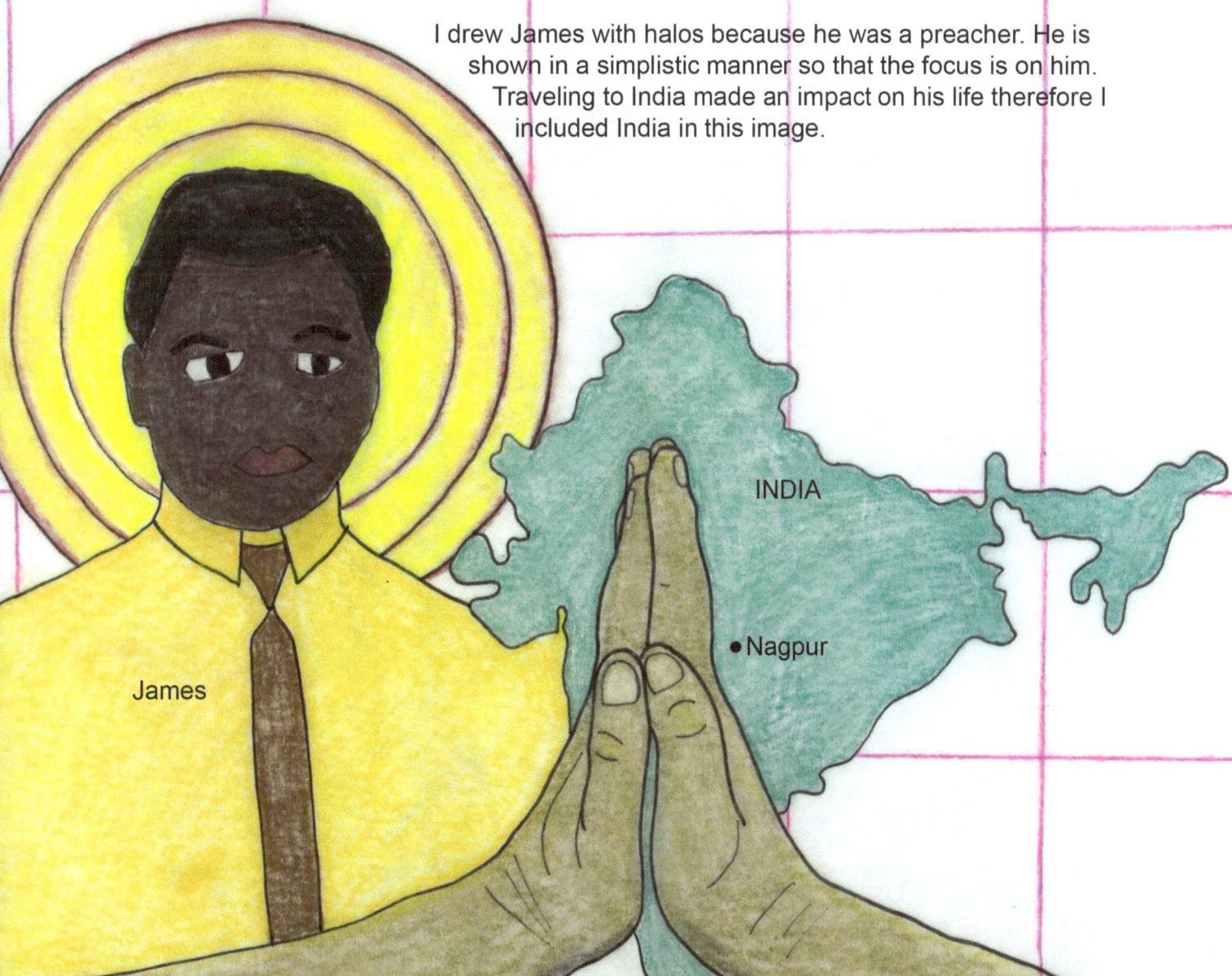

INDIA

• Nagpur

James

Leader James Chaney is combined with Artist Lois Mailou Jones because both were involved in the Civil Rights Movement and both were advocates.

James worked for all people being equal at the Congress of Racial Equity (CORE). Part of his job was to go to places where people were suffering. He would train volunteers or investigate what had happened in the location. When a church burned in Mississippi, he and two men drove for 16 hours. They arrived and were able to see the burnt church. On their way out of town, the Sheriff and the local Ku Klux Klan (KKK) members worked together to detain and kill the men. President Johnson said he would not protect Civil Rights workers but told the Governor of Mississippi that the KKK violence needed to stop.

I made James in the style that Lois might use. He has three heads because he was a CORE volunteer as well as a son and a human from Mississippi. The markings might symbolize Lois' trips to Africa. Due to the manner in which he was killed, I am giving James a hug.

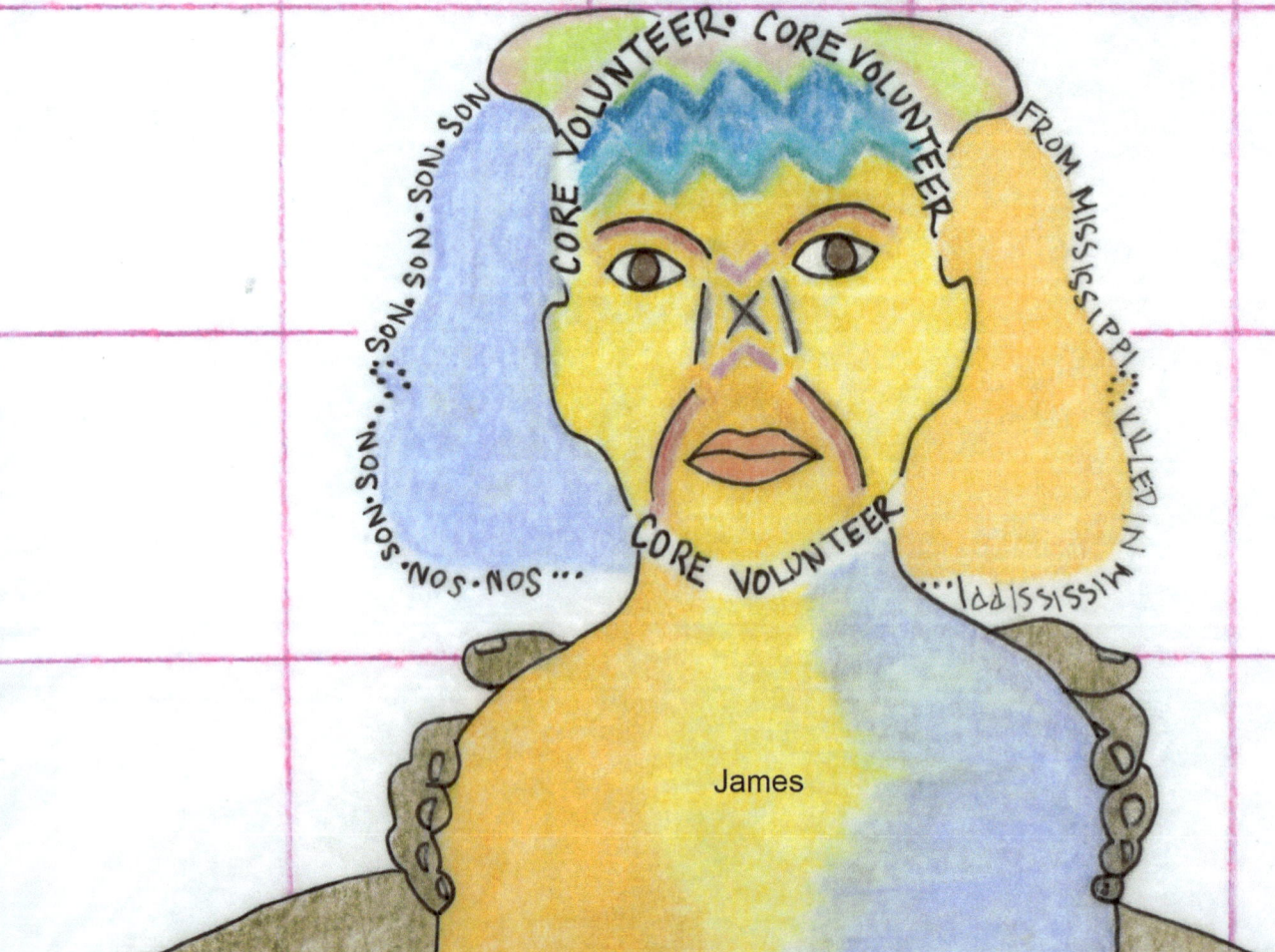

James

JACOB LAWRENCE

- USED DYNAMIC CUBISM AS A HARLEM RENAISSANCE ARTIST

- WORKED FOR THE WORKS PROGRESS ADMINISTRATION AND COAST GUARD

- MADE IMAGES ABOUT HARLEM AND THE GREAT DEPRESSION SHOWING HOW AFRICAN AMERICANS HAD TO WORK HARD FOR THE LITTLE THAT THEY HAD

I chose to show Leader Diane Nash in a style of Artist Jacob Lawrence because both were concerned about African American's equality.

Diane went to Howard University and later Fisk University. She also created the SNCC. Diane participated in nonviolent sit-ins and Freedom rides causing her to go to jail. To help the Freedom Riders in their mission of racial equality, Diane brought Martin Luther King, Jr., to Montgomery, Alabama. She helped to bring about equality in Birmingham, Alabama, and assisted African Americans in their wish to vote in Selma, Alabama.

I drew Diane in the Dynamic Cubism style where she is made of block shapes that do not show her actual features. She is surrounded by images of her life: Alabama and voting rights, and a lunch counter stool and bus.

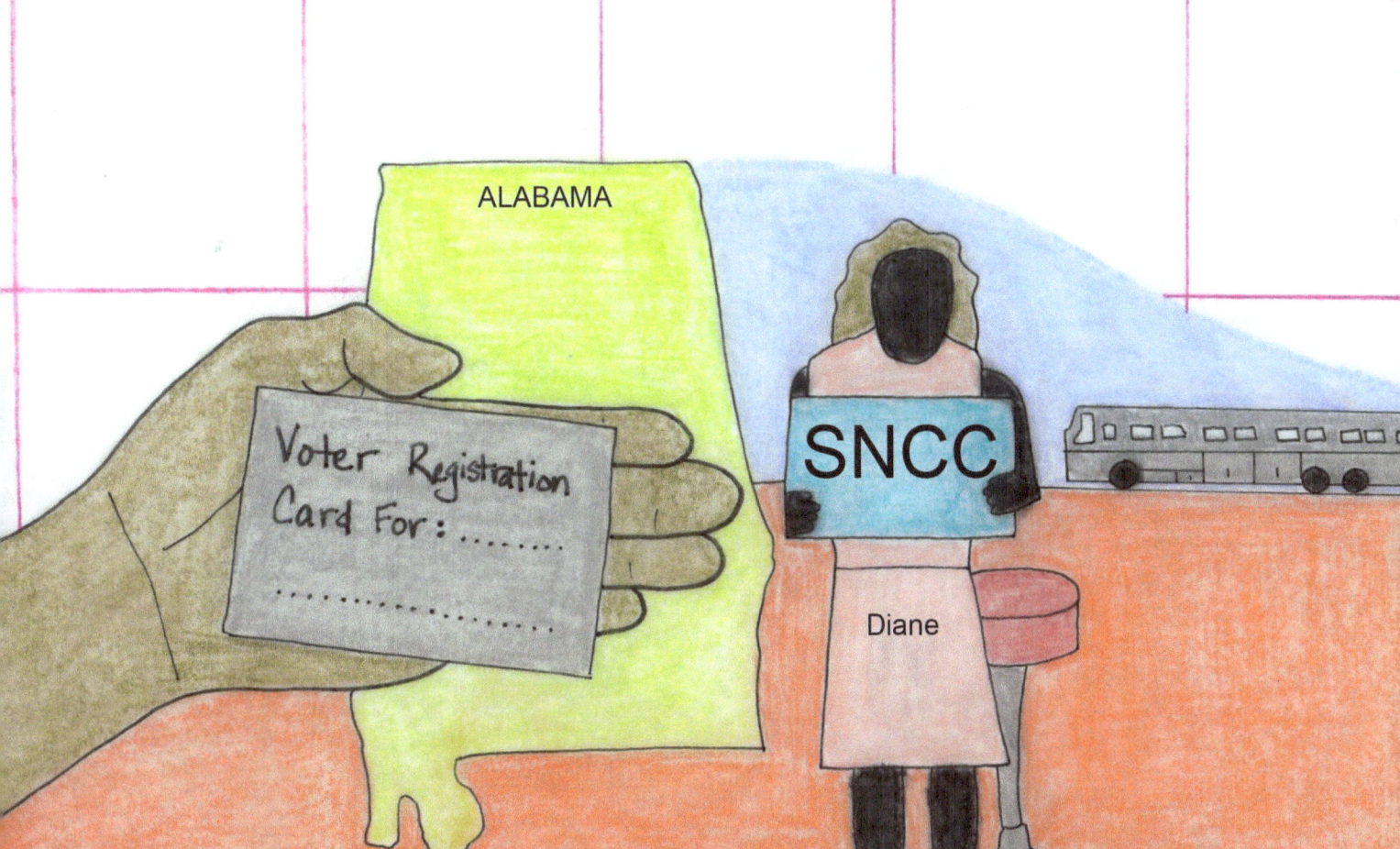

I created Leader Constance Baker Motley in a Pointillist style by Artist Georges Seurat because both people pushed the boundaries. Constance was one of the first African American politicians and Georges made art with little dots of colors that would not normally go together.

Constance graduated from Fisk University and Columbia Law School. She worked for the NAACP on cases that went before the Supreme Court. She tried ten cases and lost one due to racial discrimination that was later overturned in the 1980s. One of the cases she worked on made it possible for children in Arkansas to have equal educations no matter what their skin colors were. She was one of the first African American Senators and the first African American Federal Judge.

I sketched Constance in these colors to show that one can make a beautiful image using dissonant colors. She was able to make great strides as an African American and was not held back by her skin color. She was a judge so this half of the scale is about justice.

THIS SCALE TIPS TOWARD JUSTICE

Constance

Justice Served

Leader James Weldon Johnson is shown here as I imagine Henri Matisse would depict him. I combined this Leader and Artist because both people had many interests.

James taught high school after graduating from Atlanta University. He studied law and was a writer for a newspaper. James wrote poetry, songs for Broadway, and (with his brother's help) he wrote the song "Lift Every Voice and Sing." When he worked for the NAACP as a Field Secretary, he wanted African American schoolchildren to have the same safe classrooms as Caucasian children.

I made this half of the scale weighted down with books that represent James' interests. James is portrayed in colors that do not necessarily go together in a Fauvist or Impressionist style. I chose this style because I want the viewer to really investigate him to see what he did in his life.

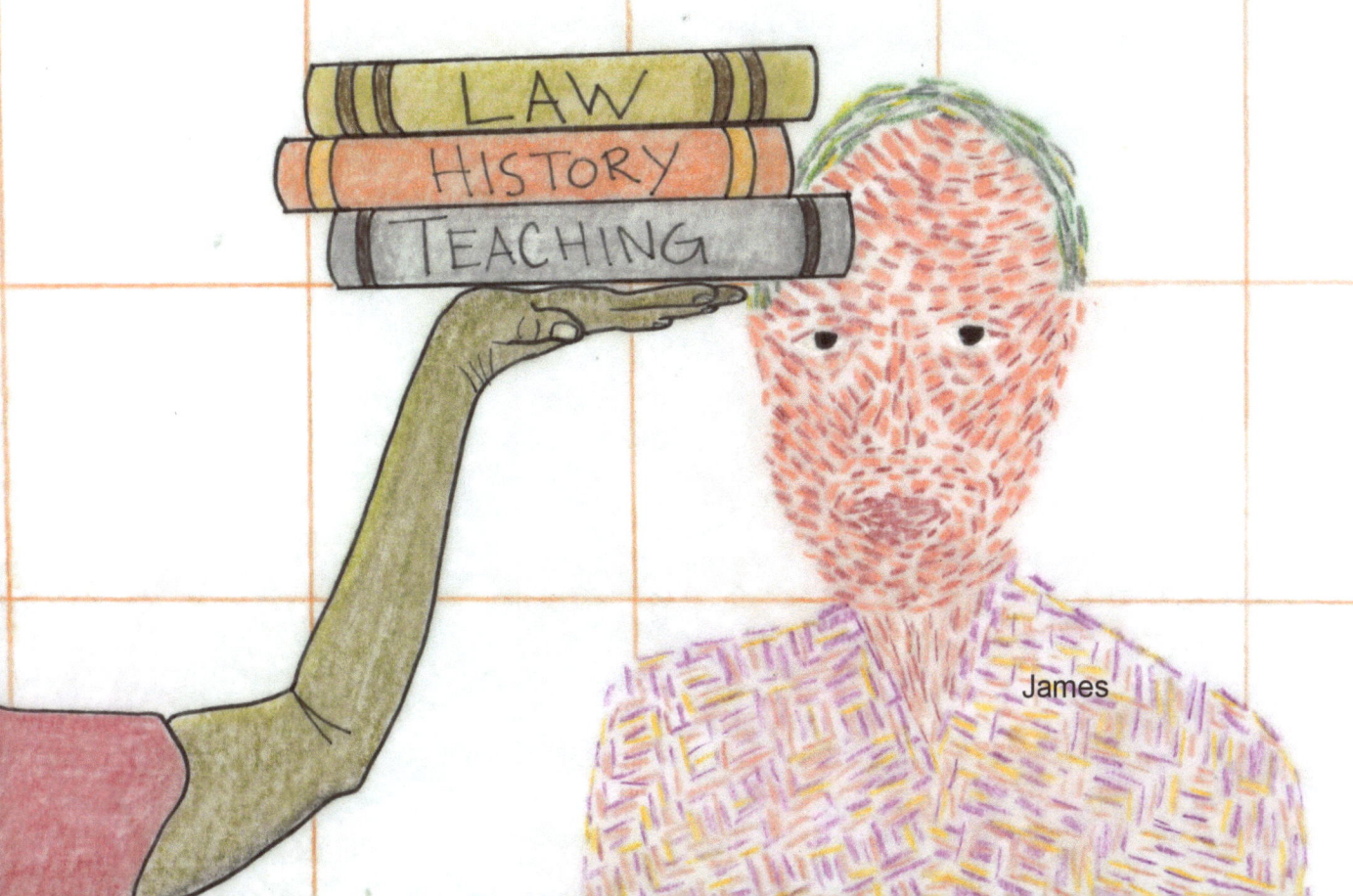

James

Leader P B S Pinchback and Artist Ernst Ludwig Kirchner are represented here because both were using bridges in their work.

P B S was born to an African American mother who had been a slave to his Caucasian father (the plantation owner). He was part of the African American and Caucasian militaries. P B S helped to make a public school system that the state would finance. He worked to ensure that everyone was equal when using public transport and when they were at businesses. He took over for the lieutenant governor, who was African American, when he died. However his political vote may have been purchased for the right price.

I chose to represent P B S in a style of Ernst because he wanted racial equality and was able to bridge the gap between African Americans and Caucasians in his political positions. His efforts helped African Americans to have more rights.

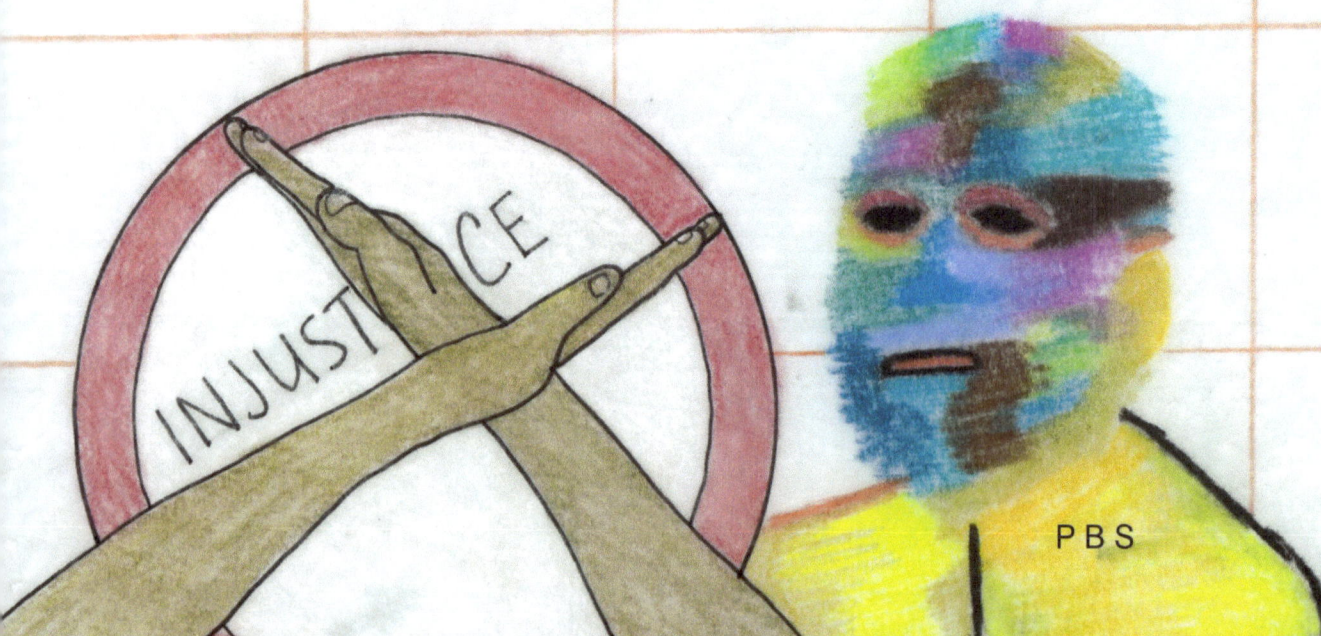

PBS

Leader Ella Baker is joined by Artist Francis Picabia because both were interested in group dynamics.

Ella was an Assistant Field Secretary and later a Director at the NAACP. She was able to organize the SNCC into a section that could focus on nonviolence and another section that could take action. She believed that groups could lead. Ella advocated for the Mississippi Freedom Democratic Party (MFDP) as well.

I am showing Ella in the Dada style with everyday items. Her hair is made from pencils. Her mouth is a ruler and it could be a metaphor for practicing non violence even when pressured to behave violently.

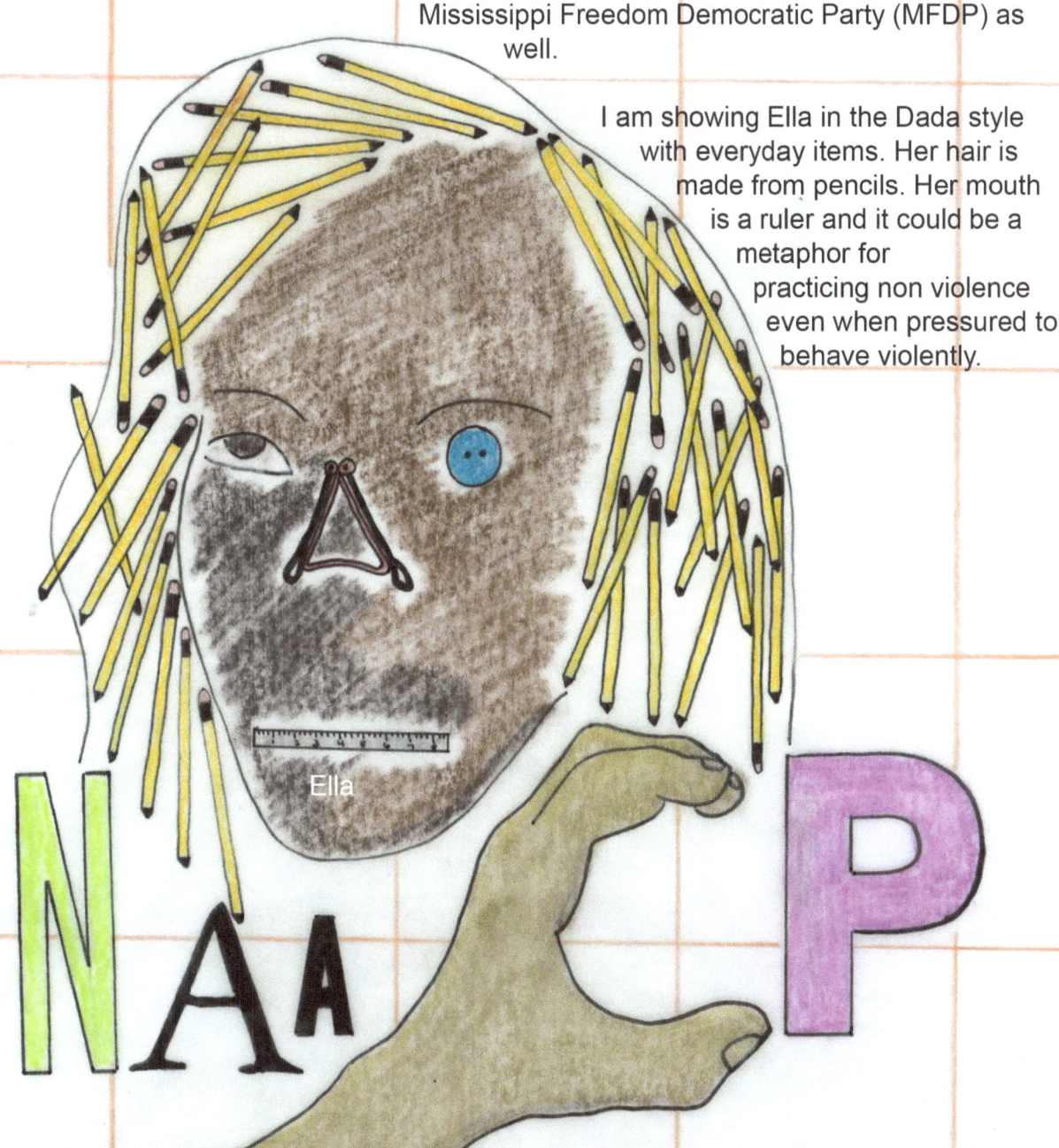

Ella

N A A P

Leader Pierre Caliste Landry is paired with Roger de La Fresnaye. Pierre was unable to continue his political work due to racism. Roger got sick and was not able to keep making art.

Pierre was born into slavery. He became a lawyer and a judge, man of the church, postal worker, school superintendent, and Louisiana politician. He was the first African American mayor, and he represented the state of Louisiana in the House of Representatives and the Senate. From the 1880s when he left his seat, until the 1965 Voting Act, there were no other African Americans represented in Louisiana politics.

I am showing Pierre in a Cubist style on the left and a more Realist style on the right. In my hand I have a microphone that Pierre could use but, just as he was passed over for future political positions due to racial inequality, the microphone is being directed to another candidate on the facing page.

Pierre

- USES RIGID AND NON-RIGID SHAPES TO MAKE PORTRAITS IN MODERN, MINIMALIST, AND POP ART STYLES
- FIGURES OUT THE GRID SO HE CAN MAKE SPECIFIC MARKS THAT ARE IN RECOGNIZABLE AND NON-IDENTIFIABLE NATURES

Leader Blanche Kelso is shown in the style of Chuck Close. Chuck works from top to bottom and left to right. I see Blanche as making a step-by-step progress from slave to politician.

Blanche was born to an African American mother who was a slave to his plantation-owner Caucasian father. He was educated with his sibling and eventually freed. After going to the Oberlin College, he helped African American children learn by starting a school for them. Blanche bought land, became a sheriff, worked as an editor at a newspaper, and was a tax assessor. He was one of the first African American politicians, a Senator. Among his other accomplishments were: Recorder of Deeds and Register of the Treasury.

Blanche

I am showing Blanche in this format because I like the way that he is both in focus and out of focus. One can see highlights and lowlights without actually seeing his features. There are hints of his eyes, ear, and mouth.

Leader Medgar Evers is shown with Artist Jackson Pollock because they were innovative.

After serving in the military, Medgar graduated from Alcorn State College. He used his time selling insurance to tell African Americans about politics and how they could join the efforts. When he applied to the University of Mississippi, the NAACP helped his cause. Later he became a Field Secretary for the organization in Mississippi. He was shot in his driveway for his efforts to end racial discrimination.

I designed Medgar in this Abstract drip style. This image also illustrates his untimely death because I am making part of his body disappear.

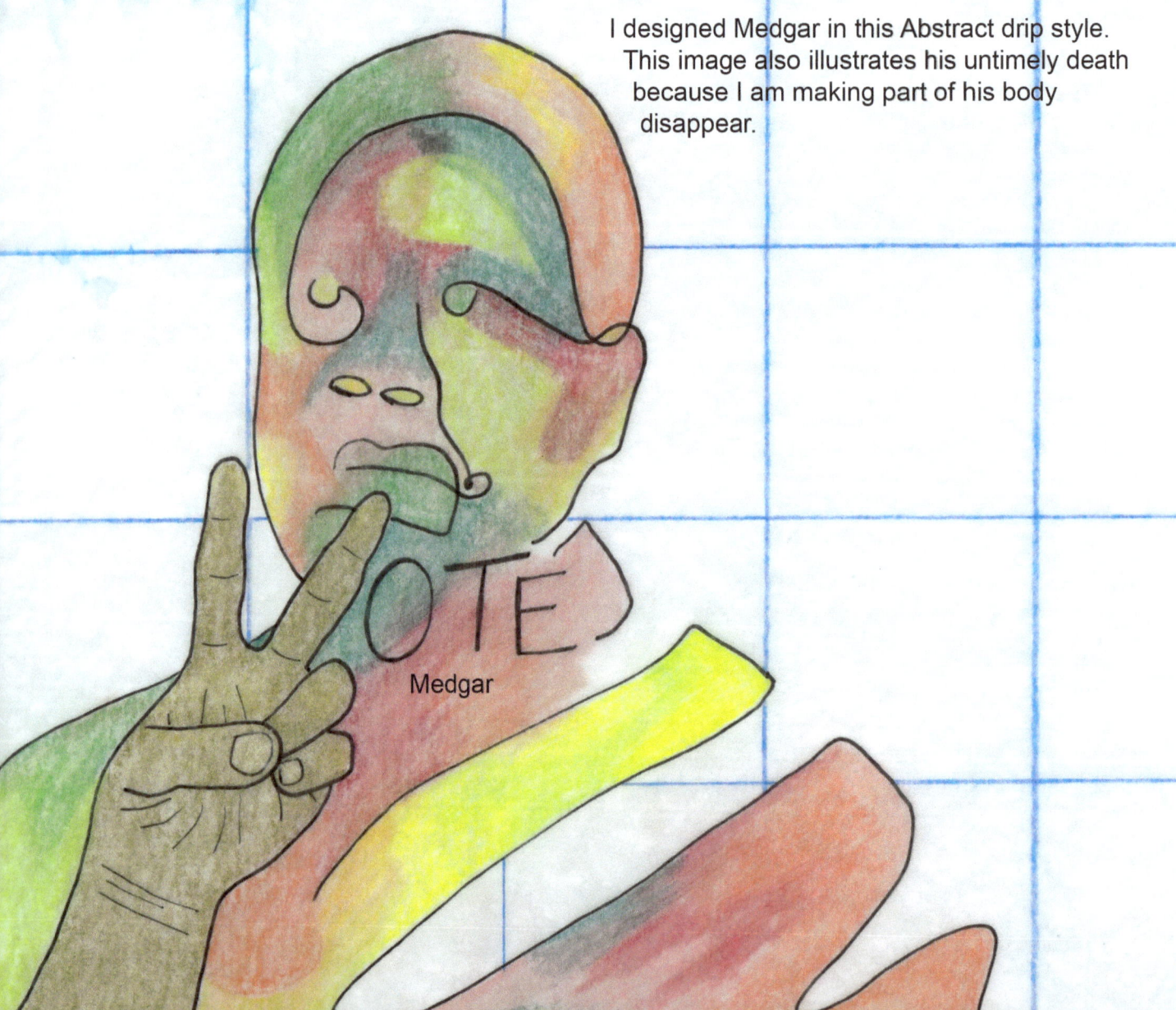

Medgar

- USES RIGID AND NON-RIGID SHAPES TO MAKE PORTRAITS IN MODERN, MINIMALIST, AND POP ART STYLES
- FIGURES OUT THE GRID SO HE CAN MAKE SPECIFIC MARKS THAT ARE IN RECOGNIZABLE AND NON-IDENTIFIABLE NATURES

Leader Blanche Kelso is shown in the style of Chuck Close. Chuck works from top to bottom and left to right. I see Blanche as making a step-by-step progress from slave to politician.

Blanche was born to an African American mother who was a slave to his plantation-owner Caucasian father. He was educated with his sibling and eventually freed. After going to the Oberlin College, he helped African American children learn by starting a school for them. Blanche bought land, became a sheriff, worked as an editor at a newspaper, and was a tax assessor. He was one of the first African American politicians, a Senator. Among his other accomplishments were: Recorder of Deeds and Register of the Treasury.

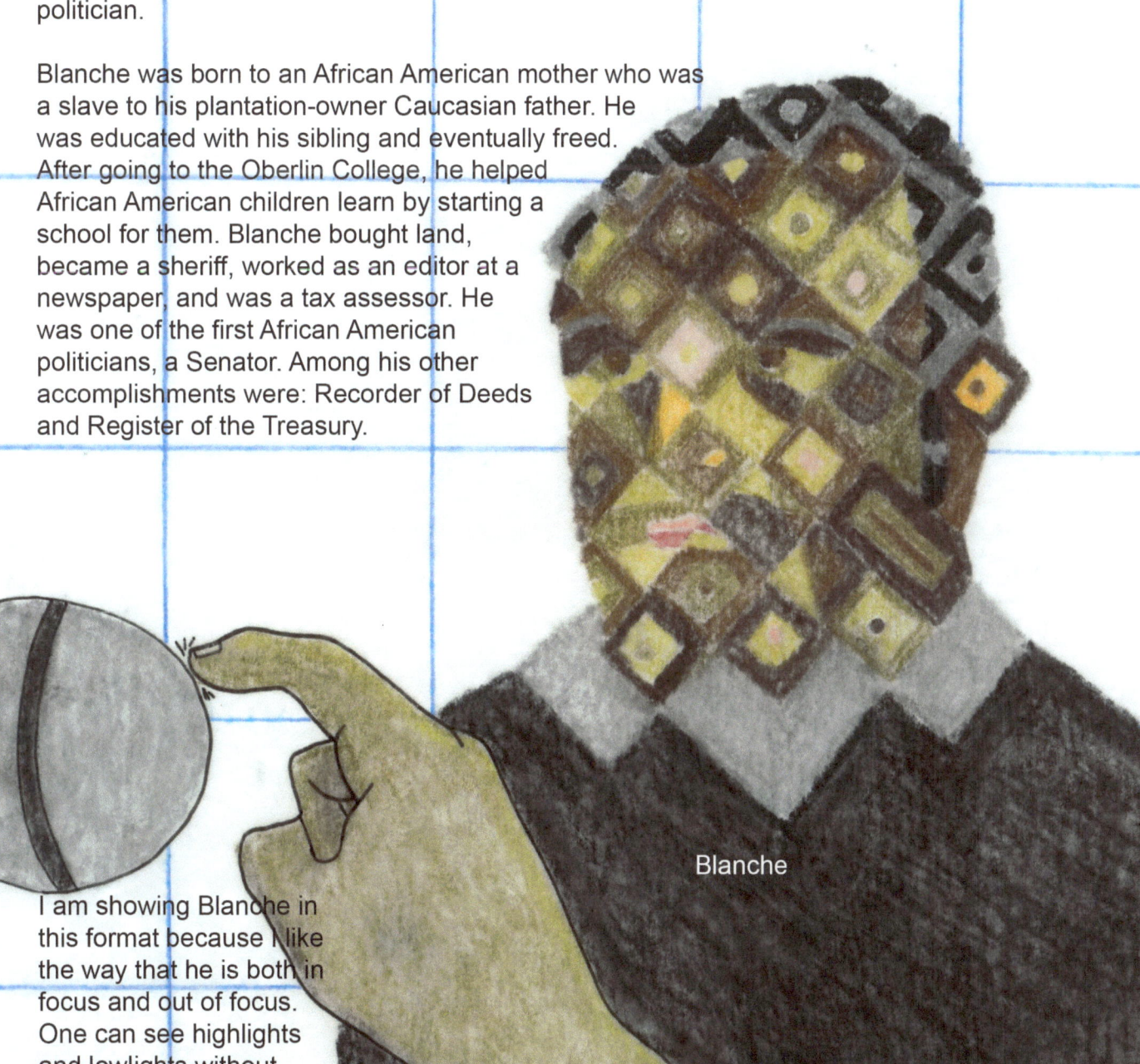

Blanche

I am showing Blanche in this format because I like the way that he is both in focus and out of focus. One can see highlights and lowlights without actually seeing his features. There are hints of his eyes, ear, and mouth.

Leader Medgar Evers is shown with Artist Jackson Pollock because they were innovative.

After serving in the military, Medgar graduated from Alcorn State College. He used his time selling insurance to tell African Americans about politics and how they could join the efforts. When he applied to the University of Mississippi, the NAACP helped his cause. Later he became a Field Secretary for the organization in Mississippi. He was shot in his driveway for his efforts to end racial discrimination.

I designed Medgar in this Abstract drip style. This image also illustrates his untimely death because I am making part of his body disappear.

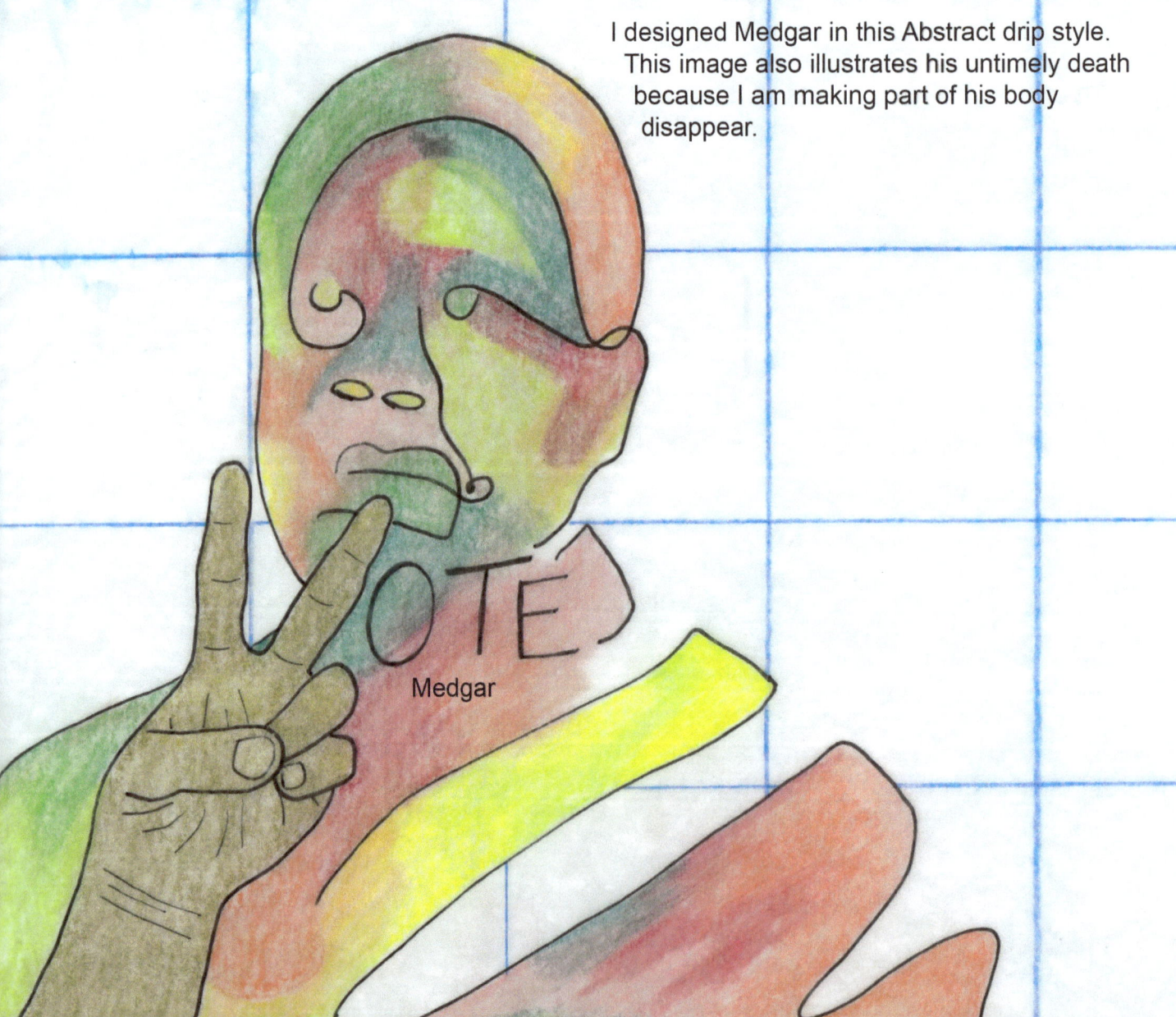

Medgar

- HAD INJURIES AND ILLNESSES BUT STILL DID WELL AT SPORTS AND INSISTED ON PAINTING UPSIDE DOWN IN HER HOSPITAL BED
- CREATED AN IMAGINARY FRIEND WHO BROUGHT HER JOY AND WAS HEALTHY
- PAINTED THAT HEALTHIER SELF AND HERSELF

Leader Vivian Malone is paired with Mexican Artist Frida Kahlo because both were strong women. Vivian was one of the first African Americans to attend the University of Tuscaloosa. After passing the entrance exam to the best high school in Mexico, Frida was one of the few girls in the school.

Vivian was an honor student and community activist who was encouraged to attend college by her parents. She started off at the Alabama Agricultural and Mechanical University but wanted an accounting degree and needed to transfer to another school for that degree. She applied to the University of Alabama. After many disputes, the National Guard made it possible for her to register for classes. Vivian was the first African American to graduate from the school.

I drew two Vivians with my hand on the calculator in between to show her graduation with an accounting degree as the first African American. Her brain is highlighted in many colors to show that she was smart. In some ways she is growing from the girl up to the graduate.

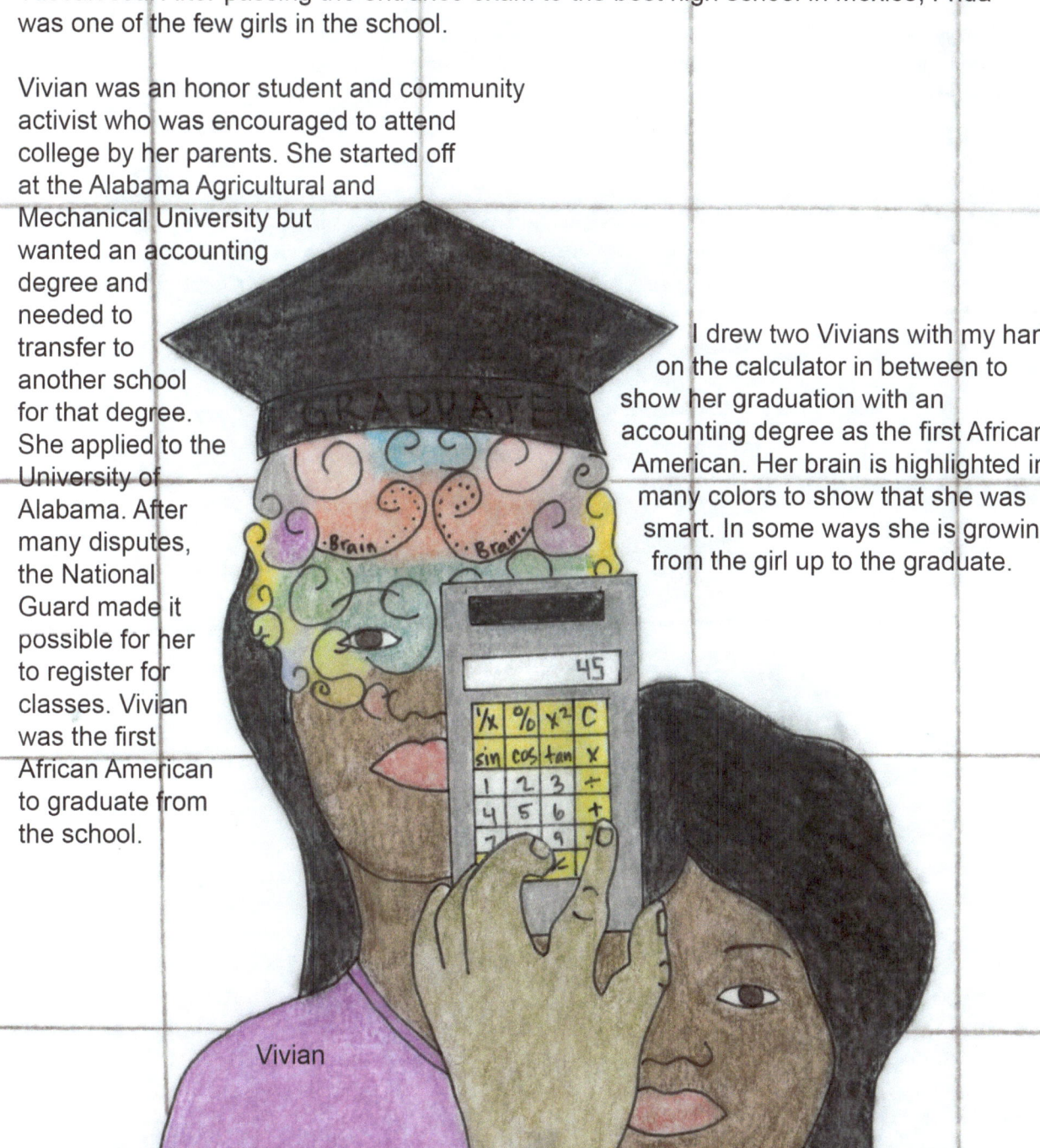

REMEDIOS VARO

- WAS FORCED TO MOVE TWICE BECAUSE OF POLITICS--ENDED UP IN MEXICO

- HAD MANY INTERESTS INCLUDING: READING ABOUT MAGIC AND MYTH, LEARNING ABOUT ARCHITECTURE AND PHILOSOPHY, CREATING AND TEACHING ART, DESIGNING BALLET COSTUMES, AND WORKING IN PUBLIC RELATIONS

Leader George McLaurin is shown in the Surrealist style of Artist Remedios Varo. I chose to combine these people because they were both exiled.

George wanted to attend the University of Oklahoma to get a Doctorate in Education. He was in his 60s and already had a graduate degree. With the help of the NAACP's lawyers, he was admitted to the University however he had to sit alone almost as an exile in a room that connected to the rest of the class. George also had to eat and study separately so he took his case to the Supreme Court. The Court removed the segregated conditions on his graduate education.

I chose to make roots growing from George's head through the book toward a Doctorate degree because it was surreal that he would have to sit in an anteroom away from his classmates. He was able to fight the law and sit with his fellow graduate students.

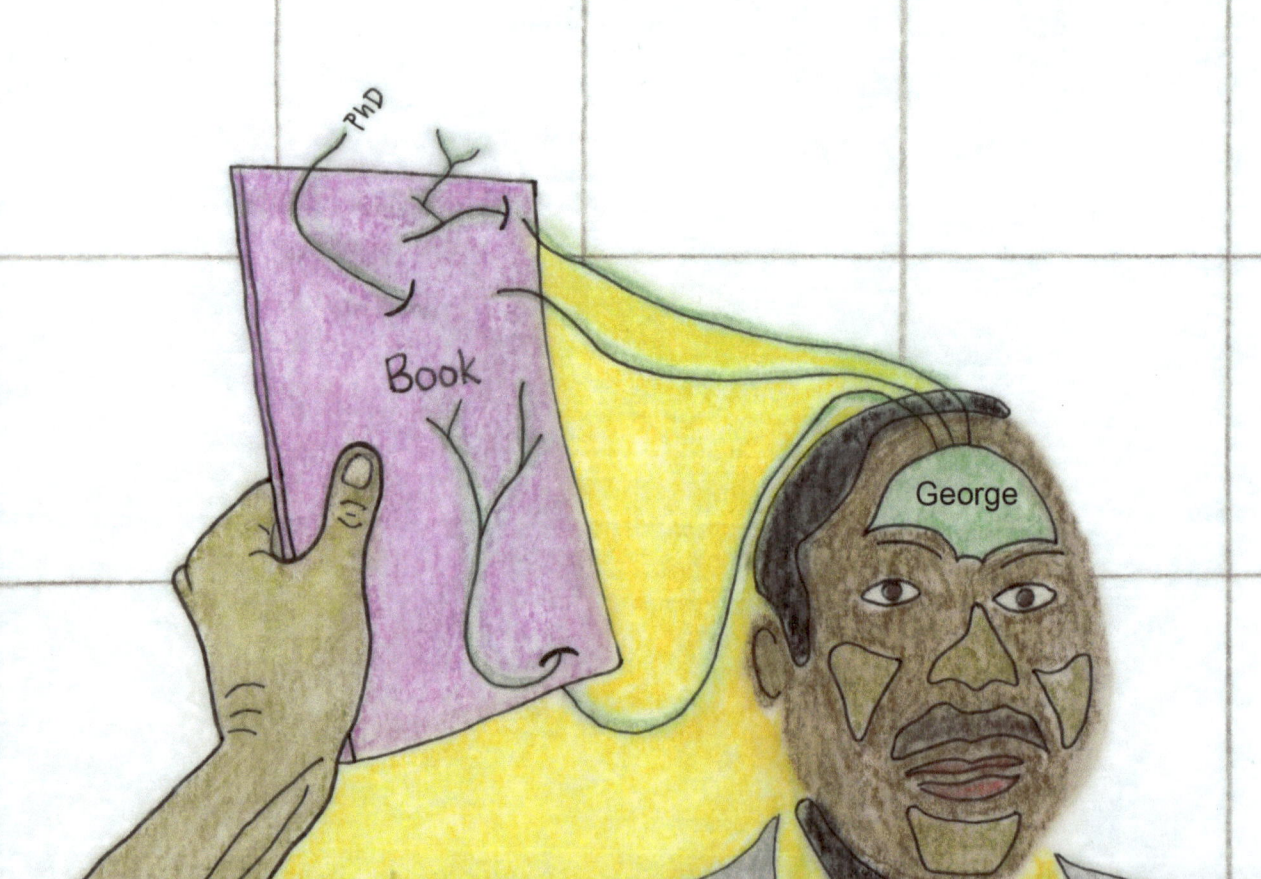

- WENT BETWEEN MEXICO CITY AND EUROPE TO STUDY ART

- LEARNED TO PAINT ON FRESH PLASTER (FRESCOES) IN EUROPE AND BROUGHT
  THE STYLE BACK TO MEXICO WHERE HE PAINTED MURALS IN PUBLIC PLACES

- WANTED HIS ART TO BE SEEN BY ALL, NOT JUST THE RICH

DIEGO RIVERA

Leader Minnijean Brown and Mexican Artist Diego are combined because they were involved in politics--Minnijean by living life, and Diego by painting life.

Minnijean was one of the nine African American students that were sent to the all Caucasian Central High School in Little Rock, Arkansas. Over 70 students wanted to attend Central, but the Superintendent did not want that many African American students so he screened them to see if they passed the personality and IQ tests. Too many passed and he told many not to come. He was left with the "Little Rock Nine." Armed soldiers escorted Minnijean and the other eight students to school.

I am representing Minnijean in a style of painting by Diego because she was an everyday girl going to high school. Her backpack is too large because it represents the Superintendent and other people who made it hard for her to get an education. Students often gave apples to teachers and I am using this apple to represent school.

Minnijean

SHIRIN NESHAT

- BORN IN IRAN AND MOVED TO CALIFORNIA TO STUDY BUT WAS UNABLE TO GO HOME DUE TO THE 1979 REVOLUTION
- MAKES IMAGES THAT QUESTION HOW MUCH POWER WOMEN HAVE
- LOOKS AT THE DRESS CODE AND CUSTOMS OF MUSLIM WOMEN

Leader Huey Percy Newton and Iranian Artist Shirin Neshat are combined because Huey was silenced as he spoke about violence and Shirin's work looks at violence and oppression.

Huey felt silenced by Oakland teachers who did not want him to be himself. He learned to read on his own using recorded text that he could read along with out of a book. Huey went to jail where he was not treated well and was only allowed to shower and exercise once every two weeks. To combat violence by police against African Americans, Huey started the Black Panthers along with his friend Bobby Seale. With their weapons, they felt they were equal to the police and able to keep the police away. The Black Panthers also assisted the poor to get health care and helped to feed African American kids. Huey got a doctorate in Social Sciences.

I chose to show Huey with the words "Black" and "Panther" on his face because of his association with the group. It is like a layer and once the viewer can see through that, she or he can question who he was and how his education and prison sentence affected him.

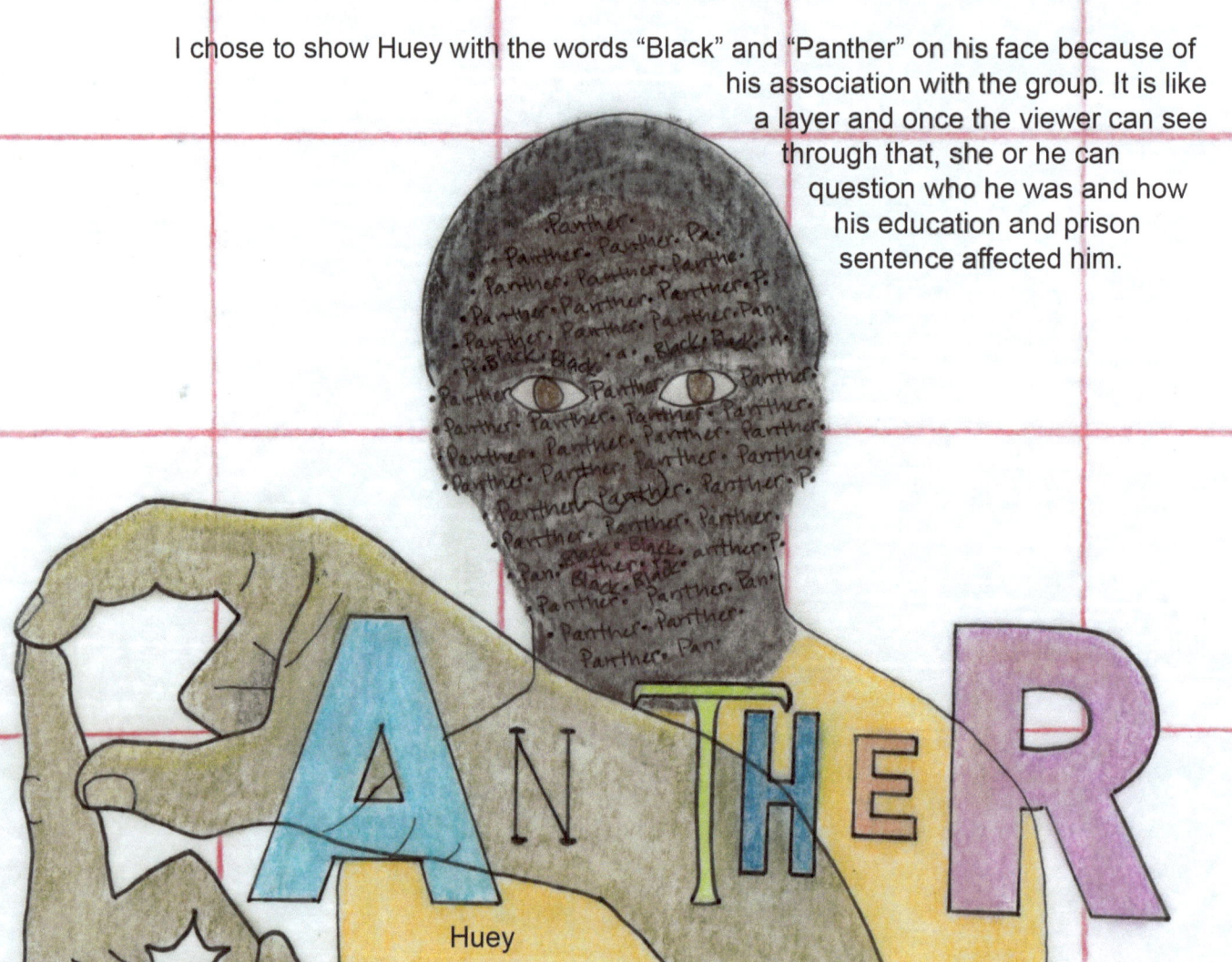

Huey

I combined Leader Ida B Wells and Iranian Artist Forough Yavari because both were refugees.

Ida was born a slave in Mississippi. A year later the President ordered that slaves should be free. Ida went to Rust University but had to drop out to take care of her siblings when her parents both died. She became a teacher. Ida wrote for her newspaper. When she started writing in the *Memphis Free Speech* about lynchings as murder and as a way to repress African Americans so they could not attain more money, Ida was forced to move due to death threats. She moved to New York City. Ida communicated political ideas to crowds in the United States and Europe.

I used the style of Forough to create images of Mississippi over Ida's face because she was born into slavery. That injustice and continued racism prompted Ida to speak out and write about better conditions for African Americans.

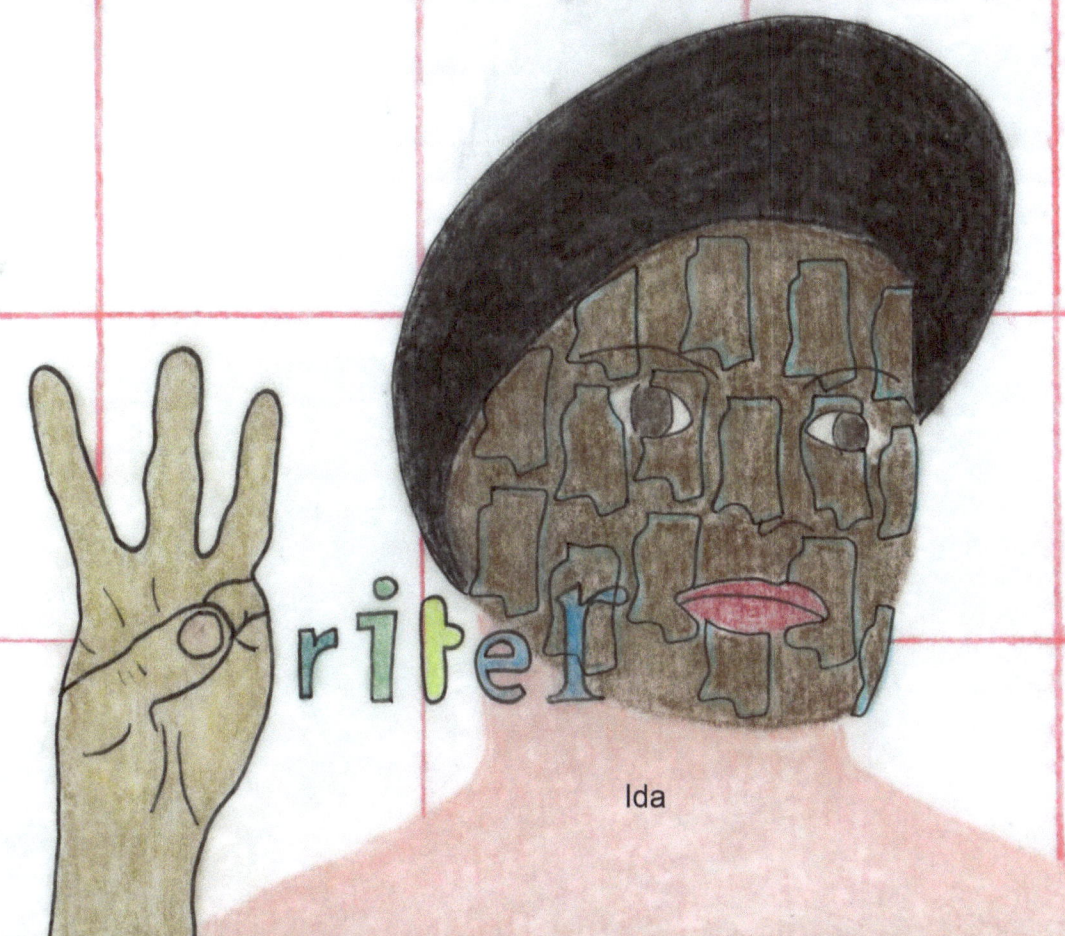

Ida

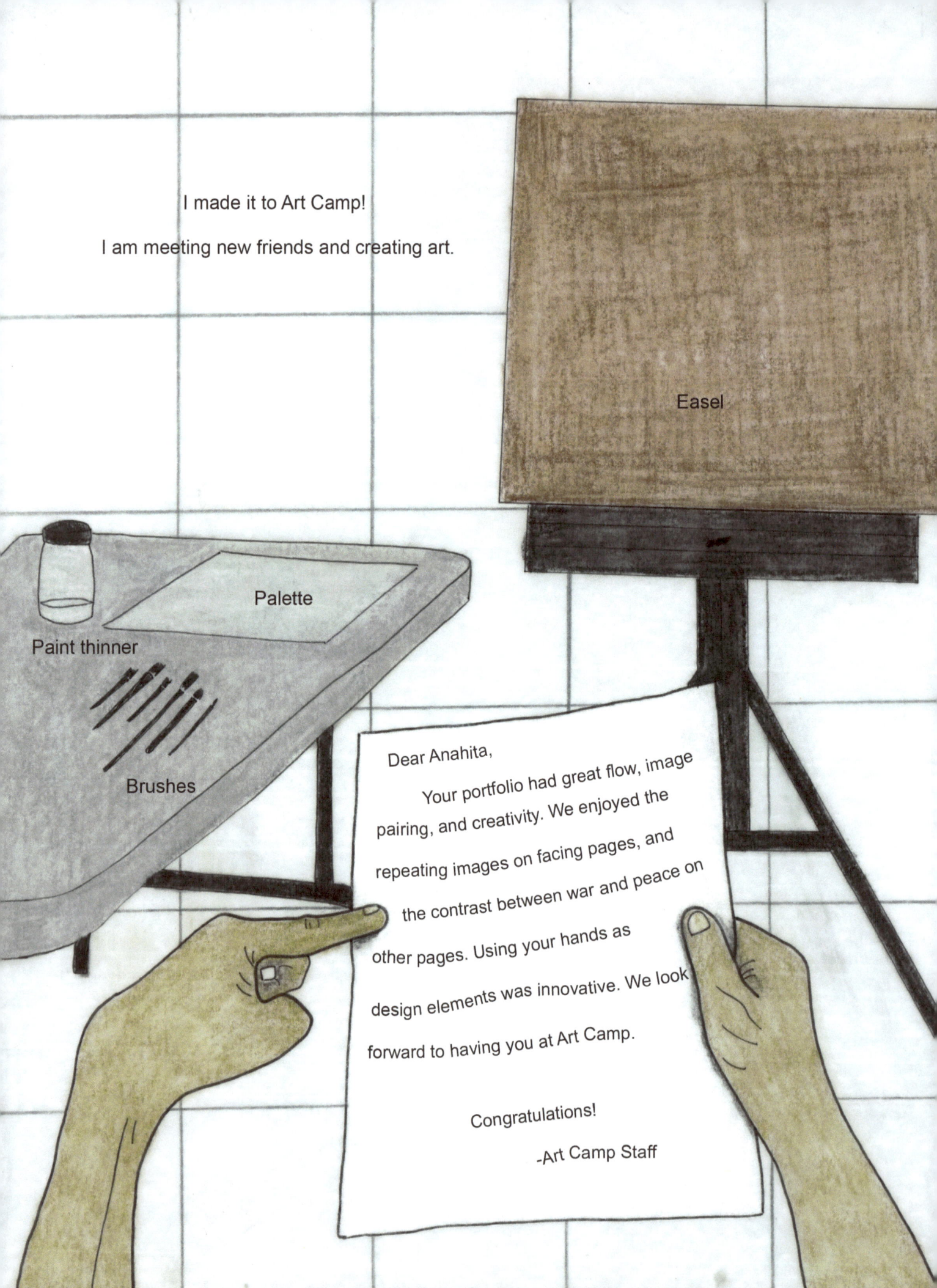

I made it to Art Camp!

I am meeting new friends and creating art.

Easel

Palette

Paint thinner

Brushes

Dear Anahita,

Your portfolio had great flow, image pairing, and creativity. We enjoyed the repeating images on facing pages, and the contrast between war and peace on other pages. Using your hands as design elements was innovative. We look forward to having you at Art Camp.

Congratulations!

-Art Camp Staff

Bibliography

Bowness, Alan. *The Book of Art: A Pictorial Encyclopedia of Painting, Drawing, and Sculpture.* New York: Grolier, 1994. Print.

Don, Nardo. *Frida Kahlo.* Detriot: Lucent, 2013. Print.

Driskell, David C., David L. Lewis, and Deborah Willis. *Harlem Renaissance: Art of Black America.* New York: Studio Museum in Harlem, 1994. Print.

Kindersley, Inc Dorling. *Art That Changed the World.* S.l.: Dk, 2015. Print.

Kleeblatt, Norman L., Maurice Berger, and Debra Bricker. Balken. *Action/abstraction: Pollock, De Kooning, and American Art, 1940-1976.* New York: Jewish Museum under the Auspices of The Jewish Theological Seminary of America, 2008. Print.

Kramer, Karen, Janet Catherine. Berlo, and Kathleen E. Ash-Milby. *Shapeshifting: Transformations in Native American Art.* Salem, MA: Peabody Essex Museum, 2012. Print.

Linton, Harold. *Portfolio Design.* New York: W.W. Norton, 2012. Print.

Rubel, David. *The Coming Free.* New York, NY: DK Pub., 2005. Print.

Rubin, Susan Goldman. *Diego Rivera: An Artist for the People.* New York: Abrams for Young Readers, 2013. Print.

Wyckoff, Lydia L. *Visions and Voices: Native American Painting from the Philbrook Museum of Art.* Albuquerque: Philbrook Museum of Art, 1996. Print.

"ABOUT R.C. GORMAN." *Biography.* N.p., n.d. Web. 20 Oct. 2015.

"Biography | Loïs Mailou Jones." *Biography | Loïs Mailou Jones.* N.p., n.d. Web. 20 Oct. 2015.

"Food And The Civil Rights Movement." *The Museum Of UnCut Funk.* N.p., n.d. Web. 20 Oct. 2015.

PBS. PBS, n.d. Web. 20 Oct. 2015.

"Forough Yavari." *Http://www.foroughyavari.com/.* N.p., n.d. Web. 20 Oct. 2015.

"Francis Picabia | Biography - French Artist." *Encyclopedia Britannica Online.* Encyclopedia Britannica, n.d. Web. 20 Oct. 2015.

"Guggenheim." *Collection Online.* N.p., n.d. Web. 20 Oct. 2015.

"NAACP History: W.E.B. Dubois." *NAACP History: W.E.B. Dubois.* N.p., n.d. Web. 20 Oct. 2015.

The Editors of Encyclopædia Britannica. "Roger De La Fresnaye | Biography - French Painter." Encyclopedia Britannica Online. Encyclopedia Britannica, 11 Aug. 2014. Web. 20 Oct. 2015.

Encyclopedia Britannica, n.d. Web. 20 Oct. 2015.